minutes. Better than real cucumber, with aloe, green tea and chamomile. For beautiful eyes.

# Six O'Clock
## SOLUTIONS

**Front cover:** Chicken Enchiladas, page 49; Southwestern Rice, page 68. Photography by Howard L. Puckett; styling by Melanie J. Clarke; food styling by Julie Christopher.

Editor: **Alyson Moreland Haynes**
Art Director: **Amy Heise**
Assistant Art Director: **Craig Hyde**
Managing Editor: **Kay Fuston**
Senior Writer: **Kate Neale Cooper**
Assistant Food Editors: **Regan Miller, L.D.; Joe Watts**
Copy Editors: **Maria Parker Hopkins, Carol Boker**
Copy/Production Assistant: **Kate McWhorter**
Food Intern: **Kristi Crowe**
Copy Intern: **Stephanie Davis**

Photographers: **Ralph Anderson, Jim Bathie, Tina Cornett, Colleen Duffley, Becky Luigart-Stayner, Randy Mayor, Howard L. Puckett**
Photo Stylists: **Cindy Manning Barr, Kay E. Clarke, Melanie J. Clarke, Virginia R. Cravens, Mary Catherine Muir, Fonda Shaia, Ashley J. Wyatt**

*Weight Watchers* Magazine Test Kitchens Director: **Kathleen Royal Phillips**
Assistant Director: **Gayle Hays Sadler** Staff: **Julie Christopher, Natalie E. King, L. Victoria Knowles, Rebecca W. Mohr, Jan A. Smith, Kate M. Wheeler**

Editor, *Weight Watchers* Magazine: **Kate Greer**
Art Director: **Jamie Ezra Mark**
Articles Editor: **Matthew Solan**
Editorial Coordinator: **Christine O'Connell**

Senior Vice President, Publisher: **Jeffrey C. Ward**
General Manager: **Vicki A. Denmark**
Business Manager: **Michael W. Stern**
Marketing Manager: **Betsey Hummel**
Assistant Production Manager: **Robin Boteler**

President and CEO: **Tom Angelillo**
Executive Vice President: **Bruce Akin**
Executive Vice President: **Scott Sheppard**
Vice President, Administration: **Jeanetta Keller**
Vice President, Corporate Marketing: **Greg Keyes**
Vice President, Consumer Marketing: **Hallett Johnson III**
Vice President, Circulation: **Pat Vander Meer**
Vice President, Magazine Production: **Larry Rinehart**
Vice President, Finance: **Bruce Larson**

Back cover: Frozen Chocolate Brownie Pie, page 87.
Photography by Howard L. Puckett; styling by Melanie J. Clarke.

## WELCOME

We no longer need to cook in order to eat. We can pick up Chinese at the take-out counter, grab a hamburger and French fries at the drive-thru, or—the ultimate food sin—buy an entire meal at a gourmet deli, hide the evidence, and pretend we made it ourselves. Yet with all these options, publishers still produce some 330 cookbooks each year.

Why bother producing so many cookbooks, you might wonder? Sure, the meals we make at home are more healthful than fast food, but the real reason cookbooks keep coming is this: Cooking isn't only about eating. Homemade meals are special in the same way that the clay ashtray your nephew made for you at summer camp (even though you don't smoke) is more valuable than the one you could buy at the mall, the same way the love letter your husband writes is more precious than any anniversary card he could buy.

There's no scientific proof to back this up, but it's common knowledge that homemade food tastes better than anything that comes in a little white box or that can be ordered from a menu. That's because a homemade meal (or ashtray or anniversary letter for that matter) imparts something that store-bought items can't impart: love.

Of course, preparing a meal at home doesn't mean slaving over a hot stove all day. *Six O'Clock Solutions* is grounded in the belief that homemade meals should be as easy to prepare as they are fun to share with the people you love. In line with that thinking, we've created 150 recipes that use shortcuts, simple ingredients, and convenience products to make homemade doable for you.

There's a Vegetable-and-Cheese Strata and a Ham-and-Lima Bean Casserole that can be made the day before you need to serve them; an orange roughy that takes only six minutes to cook; a pizza made with a refrigerated crust and staples you probably keep in your pantry; and Almond-Dusted Strawberries, a sophisticatedly simple dessert that requires a mere three ingredients.

Besides being a gesture of love, homemade food is usually more healthful than fast food or takeout. The proof is on every page of this cookbook: Each recipe includes complete nutritional information, *POINTS*, and diabetic exchanges for people who have special dietary restrictions or are weight- and health-conscious.

We've all ordered takeout instead of cooking at home—and that's okay every once in a while—but when the pizza delivery guy starts to know your kids by name, it's probably time you rediscovered one of the truly great institutions of civilized life: the homecooked meal. And with the recipes in *Six O'Clock Solutions* as your guide, you might also discover a gourmet chef within yourself.

*Alyson M. Haynes*

# Six O'Clock
## SOLUTIONS

# c o n t e n t s

# Cupboard Cooking

## THE SECRET TO FUSS-FREE DINNERS
## IS STOCKING UP ON STAPLES

*For centuries cooks have known that fruits could be preserved in jars or bottles of honey as the Romans did. Of course, today few of us have the time, patience, or know-how to "put up" our own food, but that doesn't mean we can't learn from the Romans' example. Just as canning meant they could have fruit year-round, smartly stocking your pantry with staples means you'll always have an answer to that perennial question, "What's for dinner?"*

*Cooking with pantry foods such as canned beans, veggies, and meats, grains, and pasta, and adding a fresh ingredient or two means no more daily trips to the grocery store, no more starting from scratch. By way of introduction to the concept of make-ahead, this chapter includes everything from Chocolate-Peanut Butter Swirl Cake and Sassy Black Bean Soup to Tuna-and-Wild Rice Salad and Linguine With Clam Sauce—all made with pantry staples and a few fresh ingredients. Caesar would be proud.*

**Store-bought dough and a few pantry items minimize prep time for Artichoke-and-Red Pepper Pizza.**

## Artichoke-and-Red Pepper Pizza

1   (10-ounce) can refrigerated pizza crust
    dough
Cooking spray
1   tablespoon olive oil
1   (7-ounce) jar roasted red bell peppers,
    drained and julienne-cut
1   teaspoon dried basil
1   teaspoon dried oregano
5   garlic cloves, minced
1   (14-ounce) can artichoke hearts, drained
    and coarsely chopped
1   (2½-ounce) jar sliced mushrooms, drained
1½  cups (6 ounces) shredded part-skim
    mozzarella cheese
Cracked pepper (optional)

**1.** Preheat oven to 425°.

**2.** Unroll pizza crust dough onto a baking sheet
coated with cooking spray, and pat dough into a
14- x 10-inch rectangle. Bake at 425° for 5 minutes, and set aside.

**3.** Heat oil in a nonstick skillet over medium-
high heat. Add bell peppers and next 3 ingredients; sauté 3 minutes. Remove from heat; stir in
artichokes and mushrooms.

**4.** Sprinkle half of cheese over prepared pizza
crust, leaving a ½-inch border. Spread vegetable
mixture evenly over cheese; top with remaining
cheese. Sprinkle with cracked pepper, if desired.
Bake at 425° for 10 minutes or until crust is
lightly browned. Yield: 6 servings.

*POINTS:* 5; **Exchanges:** 1½ Starch, 1 Med-fat Meat, 1 Veg, ½ Fat
**Per serving:** CAL 256 (30% from fat); PRO 13g; FAT 8.5g (sat
3.2g); CARB 30.7g; FIB 2g; CHOL 16mg; IRON 2.3mg; SOD
631mg; CALC 217mg

## Chutney-Glazed Turkey

8   (2-ounce) turkey breast cutlets
Cooking spray
¼   cup mango chutney
1   tablespoon Dijon mustard
1   tablespoon dry sherry
1   teaspoon curry powder

**1.** Place turkey cutlets on a broiler pan coated
with cooking spray; set aside. Combine chutney
and next 3 ingredients in a small bowl; stir well.
Brush half of chutney mixture over cutlets; broil

4 minutes. Turn cutlets over; brush with remaining chutney mixture, and broil an additional 3
minutes or until done. Yield: 4 servings (serving
size: 2 turkey cutlets).

*POINTS:* 4; **Exchanges:** 4 Very Lean Meat, ½ Fruit
**Per serving:** CAL 182 (15% from fat); PRO 25.5g; FAT 3.1g (sat
0.2g); CARB 11.3g; FIB 0.2g; CHOL 59mg; IRON 1.5mg; SOD
200mg; CALC 24mg

## Spicy Black Beans and Tomatoes

Substitute ¾ teaspoon garlic powder for fresh
garlic and omit the sautéeing step, if desired.

Cooking spray
1   teaspoon olive oil
3   garlic cloves, minced, or ¾ teaspoon garlic
    powder
2   (14.5-ounce) cans no-salt-added whole
    tomatoes, drained and coarsely chopped
2   (15-ounce) cans black beans, drained
½   teaspoon ground red pepper
2   tablespoons minced fresh or 2 teaspoons
    dried cilantro
Additional chopped fresh cilantro (optional)

**1.** Coat a large nonstick skillet with cooking
spray; add oil, and place over medium-high heat
until hot. Add garlic; sauté until tender. Add
tomatoes; reduce heat, and cook, uncovered, 6
minutes or until slightly thick. Stir in beans, red
pepper, and 2 tablespoons cilantro; cover and
cook 5 minutes or until thoroughly heated. Garnish with additional cilantro, if desired. Yield: 8
servings (serving size: ½ cup).

*POINTS:* 1; **Exchanges:** 1 Starch
**Per serving:** CAL 74 (12% from fat); PRO 4.1g; FAT 1g (sat 0.3g);
CARB 13.1g; FIB 4.1g; CHOL 0mg; IRON 1.1mg; SOD 233mg;
CALC 25mg

## Sweet-and-Tangy Lentils and Rice

Roasted red bell peppers, cilantro, and chutney
add flavor without fat to this meatless main dish.
Substitute ½ teaspoon garlic powder for the fresh
garlic, if desired.

1   (7-ounce) jar bottled roasted red bell
    peppers, drained and chopped (about
    ⅔ cup)
⅓   cup minced fresh or 1½ tablespoons
    dried cilantro

3 tablespoons chopped ripe olives
2 teaspoons lemon juice
½ teaspoon curry powder
2 garlic cloves, crushed
3 cups water
1¾ cups lentils
¾ cup sliced green onions
⅓ cup mango chutney
3 tablespoons honey
2 teaspoons dry mustard
3 cups hot cooked rice, cooked without
   salt or fat
Cilantro sprigs (optional)

**1.** Combine first 6 ingredients in a small bowl; stir well. Cover and set aside.

**2.** Combine water, lentils, and green onions in a saucepan; bring to a boil. Cover, reduce heat, and simmer 10 minutes. Stir in chutney, honey, and mustard; simmer, uncovered, 20 minutes or until lentils are tender.

**3.** Spoon ½ cup rice onto each of 6 plates; top evenly with lentil mixture. Spoon bell pepper mixture evenly over lentil mixture. Garnish with cilantro sprigs, if desired. Yield: 6 servings.

*POINTS:* 6; **Exchanges:** 4½ Starch, 1 Veg, ½ Very Lean Meat
**Per serving:** CAL 382 (4% from fat); PRO 18.9g; FAT 1.7g (sat 0.2g) CARB 75.4g; FIB 7.8g; CHOL 0mg; IRON 7.1mg; SOD 86mg; CALC 76mg

**Sweet-and-Tangy Lentils and Rice is ready to serve in 45 minutes.**

Spiced Peaches With
Nutty Dumplings

## Spiced Peaches With Nutty Dumplings

½ cup low-fat biscuit and baking mix (such as Bisquick)
¼ cup sugar, divided
2 tablespoons chopped pecans, toasted
3 tablespoons skim milk
⅛ teaspoon butter extract
2 cups drained canned sliced peaches in juice
⅔ cup white grape juice
¼ teaspoon apple-pie spice

1. Combine baking mix, 2 tablespoons sugar, and pecans in a bowl. Add milk and butter extract, stirring just until moist. Set aside.

2. Combine remaining sugar, peaches, grape juice, and apple-pie spice in a medium saucepan; bring to a boil over medium-high heat. Drop dough into 4 mounds on top of boiling peach mixture. Cover, reduce heat to medium, and cook 8 minutes or until dumplings are done. Spoon peach mixture evenly into 4 dessert dishes; top each with a dumpling. Yield: 4 servings.

**Note:** There are about 2⅔ cups drained sliced peaches in 1 (29-ounce) can. Store leftover peaches in an airtight container in the refrigerator for up to 5 days.

*POINTS:* 4; **Exchanges:** 1 Fruit, 1½ Starch, ½ Fat
**Per serving:** CAL 189 (17% from fat); PRO 2.6g; FAT 3.6g (sat 0.4g); CARB 38.1g; FIB 0.6g; CHOL 0mg; IRON 1.2mg; SOD 184mg; CALC 38mg

## Mushroom-and-Corn Casserole

Cooking spray
½ cup thinly sliced green onions
2 tablespoons all-purpose flour
1 (10¾-ounce) can condensed reduced-fat reduced-salt cream of mushroom soup, undiluted
1 (11-ounce) can no-salt-added whole-kernel corn, drained
1 (4-ounce) jar sliced mushrooms, drained
1 (2-ounce) jar diced pimiento, drained
¼ teaspoon pepper
½ teaspoon paprika

1. Preheat oven to 400°.

2. Coat a large nonstick skillet with cooking spray; place over medium-high heat until hot.

Add green onions; sauté 5 minutes or until tender. Remove from heat; stir in flour. Add soup, corn, and next 3 ingredients; stir well. Spoon mixture into a 1-quart casserole coated with cooking spray; sprinkle with paprika. Bake at 400° for 20 minutes or until thoroughly heated. Yield: 6 servings (serving size: ½ cup).

*POINTS:* 2; **Exchanges:** 1 Starch, 1 Fat
**Per serving:** CAL 114 (33% from fat); PRO 2.5g; FAT 4.2g (sat 0.3g); CARB 17.4g; FIB 1.1g; CHOL 0mg; IRON 0.6mg; SOD 252mg; CALC 15mg

## Tuna Melts

Melted cheese oozes down the sides of these oh-so-easy sandwiches.

1 (6-ounce) can albacore tuna in water, drained
¼ cup chopped celery
3 tablespoons light mayonnaise
1 tablespoon sweet pickle relish
2 English muffins, split and toasted
4 (¼-inch-thick) slices tomato
4 (¾-ounce) slices fat-free American processed cheese

1. Combine first 4 ingredients in a bowl; stir well. Place muffin halves, cut sides up, on a baking sheet; divide tuna mixture evenly among muffin halves. Top with tomato and cheese. Broil 2 minutes or until cheese melts. Yield: 4 servings (serving size: 1 muffin half).

*POINTS:* 4; **Exchanges:** 1 Starch, 2 Very Lean Meat, ½ Fat
**Per serving:** CAL 182 (24% from fat); PRO 15.9g; FAT 4.8g (sat 0.8g); CARB 18.7g; FIB 0.9g; CHOL 18mg; IRON 1.1mg; SOD 640mg; CALC 195mg

## Oven-Barbecued Chicken

Cooking spray
4 (6-ounce) skinned chicken breast halves
½ cup jellied cranberry sauce
¼ cup tomato paste
2 tablespoons yellow mustard
1 teaspoon cider vinegar

1. Preheat oven to 375°.

2. Line a large shallow baking dish with foil; coat foil with cooking spray. Place chicken, bone side up, in prepared dish. Combine cranberry sauce and next 3 ingredients in a blender; process until

smooth. Brush half of cranberry mixture over both sides of chicken; reserve remaining cranberry mixture.

**3.** Bake at 375° for 25 minutes. Turn chicken over; brush remaining cranberry mixture over chicken, and bake an additional 20 minutes or until done. Yield: 4 servings.

*POINTS:* 5; **Exchanges:** 3½ Very Lean Meat, 1 Starch
**Per serving:** CAL 221 (20% from fat); PRO 27g; FAT 4.9g (sat 1.1g); CARB 15.8g; FIB 0.8g; CHOL 72mg; IRON 1.5mg; SOD 188mg; CALC 32mg

## Toffee Crunch

Serve this nutty confection as candy or as a topping for ice cream or pudding.

½  cup firmly packed dark brown sugar
¼  cup sliced almonds
2  teaspoons stick margarine, softened
Cooking spray

**1.** Combine first 3 ingredients in a food processor; pulse 10 times or until nuts are finely chopped. Press mixture into a 7-inch circle on a baking sheet coated with cooking spray. Broil 1 minute or until bubbly (do not burn). Remove from oven; let stand 5 minutes. Gently turn toffee over using a wide spatula; broil an additional 1 minute. Remove from oven; let cool. Break into ½-inch pieces. Yield: 6 servings (serving size: ¼ cup).

*POINTS:* 2; **Exchanges:** 1 Starch, ½ Fat
**Per serving:** CAL 105 (29% from fat); PRO 0.8g; FAT 3.4g (sat 0.4g); CARB 18.7g; FIB 0.4g; CHOL 0mg; IRON 0.5mg; SOD 22mg; CALC 27mg

## Rice Crust Pizza With Italian-Seasoned Chicken

3  cups hot cooked long-grain rice, cooked without salt or fat
½  cup grated Parmesan cheese, divided
1  tablespoon olive oil
¼  teaspoon salt
2  large egg whites, lightly beaten
Cooking spray
1  cup canned crushed tomatoes
1  teaspoon dried oregano
½  teaspoon dried basil
¼  teaspoon salt
⅛  teaspoon pepper

1  cup drained canned sliced mushrooms
1  (5-ounce) can chunk white chicken in water, drained
¼  teaspoon fennel seeds, crushed
¾  cup (3 ounces) shredded part-skim mozzarella cheese

**1.** Preheat oven to 400°.

**2.** Combine rice, ¼ cup Parmesan cheese, oil, salt, and egg whites in a bowl; stir well. Press into a 12-inch pizza pan coated with cooking spray. Bake at 400° for 10 minutes; set aside.

**3.** Combine tomatoes and next 4 ingredients in a bowl; stir well. Spread tomato mixture evenly over prepared crust; top with mushrooms. Combine chicken and fennel seeds; stir well. Spoon chicken mixture evenly over pizza. Top with remaining ¼ cup Parmesan cheese and mozzarella cheese. Bake at 400° for 20 minutes or until crust is lightly browned. Yield: 6 servings.

*POINTS:* 5; **Exchanges:** 1½ Starch, 1 Very Lean Meat, 1 Veg, ½ Med-fat Meat, ½ Fat
**Per serving:** CAL 235 (28% from fat); PRO 15.1g; FAT 7.3g (sat 3.3g); CARB 25.8g; FIB 0.9g; CHOL 24mg; IRON 1.6mg; SOD 674mg; CALC 215mg

## Lemon Couscous

2¼  cups water
⅓  cup thinly sliced green onions
¼  teaspoon salt
1⅓  cups uncooked couscous
2¼  teaspoons grated lemon rind

**1.** Combine first 3 ingredients in a medium saucepan; bring to a boil. Gradually stir in couscous and lemon rind. Remove from heat; cover and let stand 5 minutes. Fluff with a fork before serving. Yield: 8 servings (serving size: ½ cup).

*POINTS:* 2; **Exchanges:** 1½ Starch
**Per serving:** CAL 103 (0% from fat); PRO 3.6g; FAT 0.3g (sat 0g); CARB 21.7g; FIB 0.2g; CHOL 0mg; IRON 0.6mg; SOD 74mg; CALC 3mg

## Chicken Tonnato

4  (4-ounce) skinned, boned chicken breast halves
Cooking spray
1  (6-ounce) can albacore tuna in water, drained

2   canned anchovy fillets, drained
⅓   cup plain fat-free yogurt
2   tablespoons light mayonnaise
⅛   teaspoon white pepper
1   tablespoon capers
4   medium pitted ripe olives, quartered
2   tablespoons sliced pimiento

**1.** Preheat oven to 350°.

**2.** Place chicken in a baking dish coated with cooking spray. Bake at 350° for 45 minutes or until done. Let cool completely; cover and chill.

**3.** Place tuna and anchovies in a food processor, and process 10 seconds. Add yogurt, mayonnaise, and white pepper; process 10 seconds. Place chilled chicken breast halves on individual plates, and spread tuna mixture evenly over chicken. Arrange capers, olives, and pimiento on top of tuna mixture. Serve chilled or at room temperature. Yield: 4 servings.

*POINTS:* 5; **Exchanges:** 5½ Very Lean Meat
**Per serving:** CAL 226 (20% from fat); PRO 38.9g; FAT 4.9g (sat 1.4g); CARB 4.1g; FIB 0.1g; CHOL 80mg; IRON 1.8mg; SOD 512mg; CALC 42mg

## Sloppy Joes

Serve with Sweet Potato Sticks, page 68.

Cooking spray
1½   pounds ground round
1   cup fresh or frozen chopped onion
½   cup fresh or frozen green bell pepper
1   (8-ounce) can no-salt-added tomato sauce
1   cup ketchup
1   tablespoon dark brown sugar
1½   tablespoons low-salt Worcestershire sauce
1½   tablespoons lemon juice
1½   tablespoons yellow mustard
¼   teaspoon garlic powder
¼   teaspoon black pepper
8   (1½-ounce) reduced-calorie whole-wheat hamburger buns

**1.** Coat a nonstick skillet with cooking spray; place over medium-high heat until hot. Add beef, onion, and bell pepper; cook until beef is browned, stirring to crumble. Drain in a colander; set aside. Wipe drippings from skillet with a paper towel.

**2.** Return beef mixture to skillet. Stir in tomato sauce and next 7 ingredients; cook over medium

heat 10 minutes or until slightly thick, stirring frequently. Spoon beef mixture evenly over bottom halves of buns; cover with top halves of buns. Yield: 8 servings.

*POINTS:* 5; **Exchanges:** 2 Starch, 2 Lean Meat
**Per serving:** CAL 272 (22% from fat); PRO 22.1g; FAT 6.7g (sat 2.2g); CARB 30g; FIB 2.9g; CHOL 54mg; IRON 3.2mg; SOD 673mg; CALC 43mg

## Sassy Black Bean Soup

Substitute ½ teaspoon garlic powder for the fresh garlic, if desired.

1   tablespoon olive oil
1   cup chopped fresh or frozen onion
2   garlic cloves, minced
2   (15-ounce) cans black beans, drained
1   (14.5-ounce) can no-salt-added stewed tomatoes, undrained and chopped
1   (10½-ounce) can low-salt chicken broth
½   cup picante sauce
¼   cup water
1   teaspoon ground cumin
2   tablespoons lime juice
Chopped fresh cilantro (optional)

**1.** Heat oil in a large saucepan over medium heat until hot. Add onion and garlic; sauté 5 minutes

Kids will love Sloppy Joes with Sweet Potato Sticks, page 68.

or until tender. Stir in beans and next 5 ingredients. Bring to a boil; reduce heat, and simmer, uncovered, 15 minutes. Remove from heat, and stir in lime juice. Ladle soup into bowls, and garnish with cilantro, if desired. Yield: 6 servings (serving size: 1 cup).

*POINTS:* 3; **Exchanges:** 2 Starch, ½ Very Lean Meat, ½ Fat
**Per serving:** CAL 203 (14% from fat); PRO 11.9g; FAT 3.1g (sat 0.7g); CARB 33.6g; FIB 8.9g; CHOL 0mg; IRON 3.3mg; SOD 674mg; CALC 115mg

## Linguine With Clam Sauce

2   (6½-ounce) cans minced clams, undrained
Cooking spray
½   cup fresh or frozen chopped onion
2   tablespoons minced fresh or 2 teaspooons dried parsley
½   teaspoon garlic powder
⅛   teaspoon pepper
4   cups hot cooked linguine, cooked without salt or fat (about 8 ounces uncooked pasta)
2   tablespoons grated Parmesan cheese

**1.** Drain clams, reserving juice; set aside. Coat a large nonstick skillet with cooking spray; place over medium-high heat until hot. Add onion; sauté 5 minutes or until tender. Add reserved clam liquid; reduce heat, and simmer, uncovered, 15 minutes. Stir in clams, parsley, garlic powder, and pepper; cook until thoroughly heated. Combine clam mixture and pasta in a large bowl; toss well. Sprinkle with Parmesan cheese. Yield: 4 servings (serving size: 1¼ cup).

*POINTS:* 5; **Exchanges:** 3 Starch, 1½ Very Lean Meat
**Per serving:** CAL 285 (8% from fat); PRO 17.8g; FAT 2.4g (sat 0.8g); CARB 46.5g; FIB 2.7g; CHOL 26mg; IRON 11.8mg; SOD 211mg; CALC 98mg

## Chicken Breast Dijon

For a super-quick supper, serve this entrée with steamed sugar snap peas (the frozen kind), instant brown rice, and orange wedges.

⅓   cup dry breadcrumbs
1   tablespoon grated Parmesan cheese
1   teaspoon dried Italian seasoning
½   teaspoon dried thyme
¼   teaspoon salt
¼   teaspoon pepper

2   tablespoons Dijon mustard
4   (4-ounce) skinned, boned chicken breast halves
1   teaspoon olive oil
1   teaspoon reduced-calorie stick margarine

**1.** Combine first 6 ingredients in a shallow dish or pie plate, stir well. Brush mustard over both sides of chicken; dredge in breadcrumb mixture.

**2.** Heat oil and margarine in a large nonstick skillet over medium-high heat. Add chicken, and cook 6 minutes on each side or until done. Yield: 4 servings.

*POINTS:* 4; **Exchanges:** 3½ Very Lean Meat, ½ Starch, ½ Fat
**Per serving:** CAL 192 (22% from fat); PRO 27.9g; FAT 4.6g (sat 1g); CARB 7.5g; FIB 0.5g; CHOL 67mg; IRON 1.9mg; SOD 553mg; CALC 64mg

## Tex-Mex Haystacks

1   (16-ounce) can pinto beans, drained
1   (14.5-ounce) can no-salt-added whole tomatoes, undrained and chopped
1   (10-ounce) can premium chunk white chicken in water, drained
1   tablespoon chili powder
3   tablespoons no-salt-added tomato paste
¾   teaspoon ground cumin
¼   teaspoon salt
2   cups hot cooked long-grain rice, cooked without salt or fat
½   cup (2 ounces) shredded reduced-fat Monterey Jack cheese
¼   cup thinly sliced green onions
40  baked tortilla chips

**1.** Combine first 7 ingredients in a large saucepan; bring to a boil. Reduce heat, and simmer 10 minutes or until thick, stirring occasionally.

**2.** Spoon rice onto a serving platter, and top with chicken mixture, shredded cheese, and sliced green onions. Arrange tortilla chips around outside edge of platter. Yield: 4 servings (serving size: ¾ cup chicken mixture, ½ cup rice, 2 tablespoons cheese, 1 tablespoon green onions, and 10 tortilla chips).

*POINTS:* 7; **Exchanges:** 3½ Starch, 2 Very Lean Meat, 1 Veg, ½ Med-fat Meat
**Per serving:** CAL 414 (13% from fat); PRO 28.5g; FAT 6.1g (sat 2.5g); CARB 61.8g; FIB 10g; CHOL 41mg; IRON 4.2mg; SOD 1115mg; CALC 257mg

baking sheet coated with cooking spray. Bake at 425° for 8 minutes or until lightly browned. Yield: 16 servings (serving size: 1 biscuit).

*POINTS:* 2; **Exchanges:** 1 Starch, ½ Fat
**Per serving:** CAL 99 (27% from fat); PRO 2.7g; FAT 3g (sat 0.6g); CARB 15.5g; FIB 0.9g; CHOL 14mg; IRON 0.8mg; SOD 153mg; CALC 42mg

## Vermicelli With Sweet-Hot Beef

1   pound ground chuck
½   cup water
¼   cup raisins
1½  teaspoons ground cumin
1¼  teaspoons black pepper
½   teaspoon salt
¼   teaspoon ground cinnamon
⅛   teaspoon ground red pepper
1   (8-ounce) can no-salt-added tomato sauce
2   teaspoons lemon juice
3¾  cups hot cooked vermicelli, cooked without salt or fat (about 7 ounces uncooked pasta)
Chopped fresh parsley (optional)

**1.** Cook beef in a large nonstick skillet over medium-high heat until browned, stirring to crumble. Drain in a colander; set aside. Wipe drippings from skillet with a paper towel.

**2.** Return meat to skillet. Stir in water and next 7 ingredients; cook over low heat 15 minutes, stirring occasionally. Remove from heat; stir in lemon juice. Spoon over vermicelli. Sprinkle with parsley, if desired. Yield: 5 servings (serving size: ½ cup meat mixture and ¾ cup pasta).

*POINTS:* 8; **Exchanges:** 3 Starch, 2½ Lean Meat
**Per serving:** CAL 358 (29% from fat); PRO 23.8g; FAT 11.6g (sat 4.4g); CARB 40g; FIB 2.3g; CHOL 56mg; IRON 3.4mg; SOD 280mg; CALC 29mg

## Peppered Parmesan Bread

You can substitute a 16-ounce oblong loaf of French bread for the round loaf of sourdough.

1   (16-ounce) round loaf sourdough bread
¼   cup nonfat mayonnaise
2   tablespoons grated Parmesan cheese
1½  teaspoons ground pepper
1½  teaspoons garlic powder

**1.** Preheat oven to 350°.

**2.** Slice bread vertically into 10 slices, cutting to,

---

**With ground beef in the freezer, Vermicelli With Sweet-Hot Beef can become a dinner staple.**

## Oatmeal Drop Biscuits

Dropped from a spoon rather than rolled, these biscuits have a rough, cobblestone-like appearance, and they're a cinch to make.

1¼  cups all-purpose flour
3   tablespoons chilled stick margarine, cut into small pieces
1½  teaspoons baking powder
½   teaspoon salt
1¼  cups quick-cooking oats
½   cup skim milk
3   tablespoons honey
1   large egg, lightly beaten
Cooking spray

**1.** Preheat oven to 425°.

**2.** Place first 4 ingredients in a food processor; process 10 seconds or until mixture resembles coarse meal. Add oats; process 5 seconds. Combine milk, honey, and egg in a bowl; add to flour mixture. Process 5 seconds or just until moist.

**3.** Drop dough by rounded tablespoonfuls onto a

but not through, bottom of loaf. Slice 6 longest slices in half for a total of 16 slices.

**3.** Spread mayonnaise evenly over one side of each bread slice; sprinkle with cheese, pepper, and garlic powder. Wrap loaf in foil, sealing edges. Bake at 350° for 15 minutes or until warm and toasted. Yield: 16 servings.

*POINTS:* 2; **Exchanges:** 1 Starch
**Per serving:** CAL 77 (9% from fat); PRO 2.9g; FAT 0.8g (sat 0.1g); CARB 14.7g; FIB 0.5g; CHOL 0mg; IRON 1.5mg; SOD 215mg; CALC 41mg

## Chocolate-Peanut Butter Swirl Cake

Cooking spray
1 tablespoon all-purpose flour
½ cup reduced-calorie stick margarine, softened
1¼ cups firmly packed brown sugar
1 teaspoon vanilla extract
3 large egg whites
1 large egg
1½ cups all-purpose flour
½ teaspoon baking powder
¼ cup unsweetened cocoa
¼ cup reduced-fat creamy peanut butter

**1.** Preheat oven to 350°.

**2.** Coat a 9-inch square baking pan with cooking spray, and dust with 1 tablespoon flour; set aside.

**3.** Cream margarine; gradually add sugar, beating at medium speed of a mixer until well blended. Add vanilla extract, egg whites, and egg; beat well. Add 1½ cups flour and baking powder, and beat well. Reserve 1½ cups of batter, and pour remaining batter into a bowl. Add cocoa to reserved batter; stir well. Add peanut butter to remaining batter; stir well. Spoon cocoa batter alternately with peanut butter batter into prepared pan. Swirl batters together using the tip of a knife. Bake at 350° for 30 minutes or until a wooden pick inserted in center comes out clean. Yield: 16 servings.

*POINTS:* 4; **Exchanges:** 1½ Starch, 1 Fat
**Per serving:** CAL 156 (33% from fat); PRO 3.7g; FAT 5.8g (sat 1.2g); CARB 23.1g; FIB 0.3g; CHOL 14mg; IRON 1.1mg; SOD 93mg; CALC 24mg

## Fiesta Nibbles

⅓ cup taco sauce
2 tablespoons stick margarine, melted
1 teaspoon ground cumin
1 teaspoon chili powder
¼ teaspoon garlic powder
3 cups criss cross of corn and rice cereal (such as Crispix)
3 cups crispy wheat- or rice-cereal squares (such as Wheat or Rice Chex)
2 cups tiny unsalted pretzels
3 tablespoons grated Parmesan cheese

**1.** Preheat oven to 250°.

**2.** Combine first 5 ingredients in a large bowl; stir well. Add cereals and pretzels; toss gently to coat. Add cheese; toss well.

**3.** Spread mixture evenly into a large jelly-roll or baking pan. Bake at 250° for 50 minutes or until crisp, stirring occasionally. Let cool completely; store in an airtight container. Yield: 6 servings (serving size: 1 cup).

*POINTS:* 5; **Exchanges:** 2½ Starch, 1 Fat
**Per serving:** CAL 227 (21% from fat); PRO 5g; FAT 5.4g (sat 1.5g); CARB 41.2g; FIB 2.3g; CHOL 2mg; IRON 5.1mg; SOD 474mg; CALC 51mg

## Tuna-and-Wild Rice Salad

1 (6.2-ounce) package fast-cooking recipe long-grain and wild rice (such as Uncle Ben's)
2 (6-ounce) cans low-salt albacore tuna in water, drained
1 (14-ounce) can quartered artichoke hearts, drained
1 (4.5-ounce) jar sliced mushrooms, drained
⅓ cup sliced green onions
2 tablespoons white wine vinegar
1 tablespoon olive oil
2 teaspoons Dijon mustard
¼ teaspoon pepper
8 romaine lettuce leaves
12 cherry tomatoes, halved

**1.** Prepare the rice according to package directions, omitting fat.

**2.** Combine the rice, tuna, artichokes, and mushrooms in a large bowl; toss gently. Combine green onions, vinegar, oil, mustard, and pepper in a bowl; stir with a whisk until blended. Add dress-

**Easy Chocolate-Caramel Brownies**

ing to tuna mixture, tossing gently. Serve salad in lettuce-lined dishes; top with tomatoes. Yield: 4 servings (serving size: 1¼ cups).

POINTS: 6; Exchanges: 2 Very Lean Meat, 2 Starch, 2 Veg
Per serving: CAL 298 (15% from fat); PRO 22.4g; FAT 5g (sat 0.7g); CARB 43.7g; FIB 2.3g; CHOL 17mg; IRON 3.7mg; SOD 1208mg; CALC 77mg

## Easy Chocolate-Caramel Brownies

Use a cake mix that contains pudding; the recipe won't work otherwise. Cut brownies after they've cooled. To make ahead, cool completely, wrap tightly in heavy-duty plastic wrap, and freeze.

Cooking spray
1   teaspoon all-purpose flour
2   tablespoons skim milk
27  small soft caramel candies (about 8 ounces)
½   cup fat-free sweetened condensed skim milk
1   (18.25-ounce) package devil's food cake mix with pudding (such as Pillsbury)
7   tablespoons reduced-calorie stick margarine, melted
1   large egg white, lightly beaten
½   cup reduced-fat semisweet chocolate chips

1. Preheat oven to 350°.

2. Coat bottom of a 13- x 9-inch baking pan with cooking spray (do not coat sides of pan); dust with flour. Set aside.

3. Combine skim milk and candies in a bowl. Microwave at HIGH 1½ minutes or until caramels melt and mixture is smooth, stirring with a whisk after 1 minute. Set aside.

4. Combine sweetened condensed milk and next 3 ingredients in a large bowl; stir well (batter will be very stiff). Press two-thirds of batter into prepared pan with floured hands (layer will be thin).

5. Bake at 350° for 10 minutes. Remove from oven, and sprinkle with chocolate chips. Drizzle caramel mixture over chips, and carefully drop remaining batter by spoonfuls over caramel mixture. Bake an additional 30 minutes. Let cool completely in pan on a wire rack. Yield: 3 dozen (serving size: 1 brownie).

POINTS: 3; Exchanges: 1½ Starch, ½ Fat
Per serving: CAL 122 (30% from fat); PRO 1.6g; FAT 4g (sat 1.6g); CARB 20.4g; FIB 0.4g; CHOL 1mg; IRON 0.5mg; SOD 224mg; CALC 34mg

## Peach-and-Walnut Salad

1   (29-ounce) can sliced peaches in heavy syrup, undrained and chilled
¾   cup tub-style fat-free cream cheese, softened
¼   cup coarsely chopped walnuts
6   curly leaf lettuce leaves
Dash of ground cinnamon

1. Drain peaches in a colander over a bowl, reserving ¼ cup syrup. Combine reserved syrup and cream cheese in a small bowl, and stir well. Stir in nuts.

2. Divide peaches among 6 lettuce-lined bowls. Spoon 3 tablespoons cream cheese mixture over each serving; sprinkle with cinnamon. Yield: 6 servings.

POINTS: 3; Exchanges: 1 Starch, ½ Fruit, ½ Fat
Per serving: CAL 131 (20% from fat); PRO 5.3g; FAT 2.9g (sat 0.2g); CARB 19.6g; FIB 1.1g; CHOL 5mg; IRON 0.2mg; SOD 178 mg; CALC 83mg

## Chickpea Dip

The innovative food combinations of California inspired this refreshing dip made with yogurt and lemon juice. It comes in handy for impromptu gatherings. Serve with pita triangles.

3   garlic cloves
¼   cup plain low-fat yogurt
1   tablespoon fresh lemon juice
1   teaspoon olive oil
¼   teaspoon salt
¼   teaspoon paprika
⅛   teaspoon pepper
1   (19-ounce) can chickpeas (garbanzo beans), drained

1. Drop garlic through food chute with food processor on; process until minced. Add yogurt and remaining ingredients; process until smooth. Serve at room temperature. Yield: 2 cups (serving size: ¼ cup).

POINTS: 1; Exchanges: 1 Starch
Per serving: CAL 80 (18% from fat); PRO 4g; FAT 1.7g (sat 0.1g); CARB 12.6g; FIB 3.9g; CHOL 0mg; IRON 0.3mg; SOD 41mg; CALC 9mg

# Homemade Head Starts

PREPARING DISHES AHEAD OF TIME IS A
GREAT WAY TO GUARANTEE A HEALTHFUL
MEAL IN A HURRY.

*We need healthful habits the most when our lives are busy and demanding, but it's times like these when the promises we've made to ourselves are the hardest to keep. Our eating habits probably suffer the most. Unfortunately, it is during our typically slower weekends, not on busy weeknights, that we have time to cook. But there is a way to eat fast without eating fast food. This chapter will show you how to prepare meals ahead so they're ready to serve when you're pressed for time. You can freeze our Chunky Vegetable Soup until a chilly evening when you need a warm bowl of homemade comfort. Steak With Ale marinates all afternoon while you run errands; throw it on the grill when you're ready to eat. And Mama's Chicken Stew simmers while you're at work. Just knowing that a good dinner is waiting for you at home will do wonders for your stress level.*

**Full of vegetables and grains, Beef-and-Pasta Stew is a complete meal.**

## Beef-and-Pasta Stew

4   cups water
2   cups chopped onion
1½  cups quartered small red potatoes
1   cup dried Great Northern or navy beans
½   cup sliced carrot
½   cup quartered mushrooms
½   cup uncooked pearl barley
½   pound lean, boned round steak, cut into
    ½-inch pieces
1   (14.5-ounce) can pasta-style chunky
    tomatoes, undrained
1   (14¼-ounce) can fat-free beef broth
3   garlic cloves, chopped
1   cup sliced zucchini
1   cup torn fresh spinach
½   cup uncooked ziti (short tubular pasta)
1   tablespoon dried rosemary, crushed
1   teaspoon salt
1   teaspoon rubbed sage
½   teaspoon pepper
¼   teaspoon ground nutmeg
½   cup grated Parmesan cheese

**1.** Combine first 11 ingredients in a large electric slow-cooker. Cover with lid, and cook on high-heat setting for 6 hours. Add zucchini and next 7 ingredients; cover and cook on high-heat setting an additional 30 minutes or until beans are tender. Ladle into individual soup bowls, and sprinkle with cheese. Yield: 8 servings (serving size: 1½ cups stew and 1 tablespoon cheese).

*POINTS:* 5; **Exchanges:** 1 Lean Meat, 2 Starch, 3 Veg
**Per serving:** CAL 287 (11% from fat); PRO 18.7g; FAT 3.6g (sat 1.6g); CARB 45.6g; FIB 7.3g; CHOL 20mg; IRON 4.5mg; SOD 503mg; CALC 168mg

## Milwaukee Sweet-Tart Supper

Make-Ahead Tip: Place the ingredients in the slow-cooker after lunch, and then dinner will be ready about four hours later.

1½  pounds low-fat turkey kielbasa, cut into
    3-inch pieces and divided
3   (10-ounce) cans Bavarian-style sauerkraut,
    rinsed and drained
3   large Granny Smith apples, peeled, cored,
    and cut crosswise into rings
1   medium onion, thinly sliced and separated
    into rings
1   (14¼-ounce) can fat-free chicken broth

½   teaspoon caraway seeds
8   medium red potatoes (about 3½ pounds),
    peeled and quartered
¼   cup (1 ounce) shredded Swiss cheese

**1.** Place half of sausage in an electric slow-cooker, and top with sauerkraut, remaining sausage, apple rings, and onion rings. Pour chicken broth over mixture, and sprinkle with caraway seeds. Cover with lid, and cook on high-heat setting for 4 hours or until apples and onion are tender.
**2.** Place potatoes in a saucepan, and cover with water; bring to a boil. Reduce heat, and simmer 20 minutes or until tender; drain.
**3.** Arrange sausage mixture and potatoes on individual plates, and sprinkle cheese over sausage mixture. Yield: 8 servings (serving size: 1½ cups sausage mixture, 1 cup potatoes, and 1½ teaspoons cheese).

*POINTS:* 6; **Exchanges:** 2 Starch, 1 Fruit, 1 Veg, 1 Med-fat Meat
**Per serving:** CAL 323 (25% from fat); PRO 16.1g; FAT 8.9g (sat 2.9g); CARB 52.8g; FIB 8.2g; CHOL 48mg; IRON 10.7mg; SOD 1,213mg; CALC 51mg

## Easy Crock-Pot Chicken

6   chicken drumsticks (about 1½ pounds),
    skinned
6   chicken thighs (about 3 pounds),
    skinned
⅓   cup dry white wine
¼   cup instant chopped onion flakes
2   teaspoons chicken-flavored bouillon
    granules
½   teaspoon dried Italian seasoning
½   teaspoon salt-free lemon-herb seasoning
¼   teaspoon garlic powder
¼   teaspoon dried tarragon
¼   teaspoon crushed red pepper
1   (14.5-ounce) can no-salt-added stewed
    tomatoes, undrained and chopped
6   cups hot cooked rice, without salt or fat

**1.** Trim fat from chicken. Place chicken in an electric slow-cooker; stir in wine and next 8 ingredients. Cover with lid, and cook on high-heat setting for 1 hour. Reduce heat setting to low, and cook for 3½ hours. Serve over rice.

Yield: 6 servings (serving size: 1 chicken drum-stick, 1 chicken thigh, about ½ cup sauce, and 1 cup rice).

**POINTS**: 10; **Exchanges**: 3½ Starch, 4½ Very Lean Meat, 1 Veg, ½ Fat.
**Per serving**: CAL 493 (14% from fat); PRO 44.4g; FAT 7.9g (sat 2g); CARB 57.7g; FIB 1.2g; CHOL 158 mg; IRON 4.7mg; SOD 462mg; CALC 76mg

## Tuna Romanoff

Make-Ahead Tip: You can assemble the casserole up to four hours ahead of time, omitting bread-crumb mixture. Cover and chill; then let stand at room temperature 30 minutes before baking. Top with breadcrumb mixture during last 10 minutes of baking.

Cooking spray
1   cup presliced fresh mushrooms
1   cup chopped onion
⅓   cup sliced celery
1   small garlic clove, minced
¾   cup 1% low-fat milk
¼   cup grated Parmesan cheese
¼   cup light mayonnaise
½   teaspoon dried dill
¼   teaspoon salt
¼   teaspoon pepper
1   (10¾-ounce) can condensed reduced-fat reduced-salt cream of celery soup, undiluted
3½ cups hot cooked medium egg noodles (about 2¼ cups uncooked), cooked without salt or fat
1   cup frozen green peas
1   (9-ounce) can tuna in water, drained
1   (2-ounce) jar diced pimiento, drained
¼   cup dry breadcrumbs
¼   cup grated Parmesan cheese
1   tablespoon stick margarine, melted

**1.** Preheat oven to 350°.

**2.** Coat a nonstick skillet with cooking spray; place over medium heat until hot. Add mush-rooms and next 3 ingredients; sauté until tender.

**3.** Combine milk and next 6 ingredients in a bowl; stir well. Add mushroom mixture, noodles, and next 3 ingredients; stir gently.

**A slice of brown bread and Milwaukee Sweet-Tart Supper make a hearty meal.**

**4.** Spoon noodle mixture into a shallow 2-quart casserole coated with cooking spray. Cover and bake at 350° for 40 minutes.

**5.** Combine breadcrumbs, ¼ cup Parmesan cheese, and margarine in a bowl; stir and sprinkle over casserole. Bake, uncovered, an additional 10 minutes. Yield: 6 servings (serving size: 1 cup).

*POINTS:* 7; **Exchanges:** 2½ Starch, 1½ Fat, 1½ Very Lean Meat, ½ Lean Meat
**Per serving:** CAL 336 (28% from fat); PRO 20.1g; FAT 10.5g (sat 2.8g); CARB 39.6g; FIB 4.1g; CHOL 57mg; IRON 2.8mg; SOD 741mg; CALC 164mg

### Simple Chicken Fajitas

Make-Ahead Tip: When you only have a short time to prepare dinner, these fajitas can be on the table in 20 minutes. A few minutes spent on the marinade in the morning means a flavor-packed dinner is minutes away in the evening.

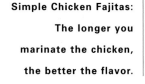

**Simple Chicken Fajitas: The longer you marinate the chicken, the better the flavor.**

    2   tablespoons balsamic vinegar
    1   tablespoon lemon juice
    2   teaspoons olive oil
    ½   teaspoon dried oregano
    2   (4-ounce) skinned, boned chicken breast
        halves
Cooking spray
    2   curly leaf lettuce leaves
    2   tablespoons salsa
    2   (6-inch) flour tortillas
Red onion rings (optional)
Fresh oregano (optional)

**1.** Combine first 5 ingredients in a zip-top plastic bag; seal and marinate in refrigerator 8 hours. Remove chicken from bag; discard marinade. Place chicken on a broiler pan coated with cooking spray; broil 8 minutes on each side or until done. Divide chicken, lettuce, and salsa evenly between tortillas; roll up. Garnish with onion and oregano, if desired. Yield: 2 servings.

*POINTS:* 6; **Exchanges:** 3½ Very Lean Meat, 1½ Starch, 1 Fat
**Per serving:** CAL 276 (22% from fat); PRO 29.8g; FAT 6.7g (sat 1.4g); CARB 21.1g; FIB 1.6g; CHOL 72mg; IRON 2.3mg; SOD 304mg; CALC 69mg

## Make-Ahead Cheese-and-Hamburger Casserole

Make-Ahead Tips: The penne does not have to be cooked beforehand because it absorbs the liquid when refrigerated overnight. If you want to make it the same day, cook the pasta before combining with all the ingredients. For convenience, use precrumbled feta and preshredded mozzarella.

1    pound ground round
1    cup chopped onion
3    garlic cloves, crushed
1    (8-ounce) package presliced fresh
     mushrooms
6    tablespoons tomato paste
1    teaspoon sugar
1    teaspoon dried thyme
1    teaspoon dried oregano
¼    teaspoon pepper
1    (28-ounce) can whole tomatoes,
     undrained and chopped
⅓    cup all-purpose flour
2½   cups 2% reduced-fat milk
1    cup (4 ounces) crumbled feta cheese
¾    cup (3 ounces) shredded part-skim
     mozzarella cheese
4    cups uncooked penne (tubular-shaped pasta)
1    tablespoon chopped fresh parsley
     (optional)

**1.** Combine ground round, onion, and garlic in a large nonstick skillet, and cook over medium-high heat until beef is browned, stirring to crumble. Add mushrooms, and cook 5 minutes or until tender. Add tomato paste and next 5 ingredients, and stir well. Bring mixture to a boil; reduce heat, and simmer, uncovered, 20 minutes. Set aside.

**2.** Place flour in a medium saucepan. Gradually add milk, stirring with a whisk until blended. Place over medium heat; cook 10 minutes or until thick, stirring constantly. Stir in cheeses; cook 3 minutes or until cheeses melt, stirring constantly. Reserve ½ cup cheese sauce. Pour remaining cheese sauce, beef mixture, and pasta into a 13- x 9-inch baking dish, and stir gently. Drizzle reserved cheese sauce over pasta mixture. Cover and refrigerate 24 hours.

**3.** Preheat oven to 350°.

**4.** Bake at 350°, covered, for 1 hour and 10 minutes or until thoroughly heated and pasta is tender; sprinkle with fresh parsley, if desired. Yield: 8 servings.

*POINTS*: 9; **Exchanges:** 2 Starch, 1 Low-Fat Milk, 2 Veg, 1½ Lean Meat.
**Per serving:** CAL 412 (23% from fat); PRO 27.5g; FAT 10.8g (sat 5.5g); CARB 51.1g; FIB 3.2g; CHOL 60mg; IRON 4.9mg; SOD 448mg; CALC 286mg

## Beef Potpie

Make-Ahead Tip: You can assemble the casserole ahead of time, without thawing the frozen vegetables and by omitting the biscuits. Cover and freeze. Then thaw the frozen casserole overnight in refrigerator; let stand at room temperature 30 minutes. Top with biscuits, and bake as directed.

½    cup all-purpose flour
¼    cup nonfat dry milk
1    teaspoon dry mustard
1    cup water
1    tablespoon Worcestershire sauce
1    (10½-ounce) can beef broth
1    pound ultra-lean ground beef
1    cup chopped onion
Cooking spray
1    tablespoon dried parsley
½    teaspoon garlic powder
½    teaspoon pepper
¼    teaspoon dried thyme
1    (16-ounce) package frozen New England-
     style sweet peas, potatoes, and carrots,
     thawed
1    (6-ounce) jar sliced mushrooms, drained
1    (4.5-ounce) can refrigerated buttermilk
     biscuits

**1.** Preheat oven to 400°.

**2.** Combine first 3 ingredients in a large bowl, and stir well. Gradually add water, Worcestershire sauce, and broth, stirring with a whisk until blended; set aside.

**3.** Cook beef and onion in a large saucepan coated with cooking spray over medium-high heat until browned, stirring to crumble. Drain well; return meat mixture to pan. Add parsley and next 5 ingredients; stir well. Add broth mixture; cook over medium heat 15 minutes or until thick, stirring constantly.

**4.** Spoon mixture into a 13- x 9-inch baking dish coated with cooking spray. Carefully split uncooked biscuits in half horizontally; place biscuit halves over meat mixture. Bake at 400° for 10 minutes or until biscuits are lightly browned. Yield: 6 servings (serving size: about 1 cup beef mixture and 2 biscuit halves).

POINTS: 6; **Exchanges:** 2½ Starch, 2½ Very Lean Meat
**Per serving:** CAL 293 (21% from fat); PRO 23.4g; FAT 6.8g (sat 2.1g); CARB 37.6g; FIB 0.9g; CHOL 59mg; IRON 2.9mg; SOD 778mg; CALC 91mg

## Shredded Beef Sandwiches

Make-Ahead Tip: Cooked in an electric slow-cooker, this recipe is perfect for a busy day. It produces its own "au jus," a delicious hot dip for the sandwiches.

1   (3¼-pound) lean, boned chuck roast
⅓   cup white vinegar
½   teaspoon salt
¼   teaspoon ground cloves
⅛   teaspoon garlic powder
1   large onion, cut into 8 wedges
3   bay leaves
9   (1½-ounce) hamburger buns, split
9   lettuce leaves

*Shredded Beef Sandwiches will become a family favorite.*

**1.** Trim fat from roast. Place roast and next 6 ingredients in an electric slow-cooker. Cover with lid; cook over low-heat setting for 11 hours or until roast is tender. Remove roast from slow-cooker; let stand 10 minutes. Shred with 2 forks, and set aside.

**2.** Strain cooking liquid; discard solids. Cover liquid, and freeze at least 1 hour. Skim solidified fat from surface; discard. Place cooking liquid in a saucepan, and bring to a boil; remove from heat.

**3.** Line bottom halves of buns with lettuce leaves; top evenly with shredded beef and top halves of buns. Serve hot cooking liquid as a dipping sauce. Yield: 9 servings.

POINTS: 7; **Exchanges:** 4 Lean Meat, 1½ Fat
**Per serving:** CAL 324 (26% from fat); PRO 32.2g; FAT 9.4g (sat 3.5g); CARB 24.5g; FIB 1.2g; CHOL 87mg; IRON 4.3mg; SOD 435mg; CALC 31mg

## Slow-Cooker Beef-and-Bean Burritos

Make-Ahead Tip: Since the meat cooks slowly throughout the day, all you have to do at dinnertime is assemble the burritos.

1   (2-pound) top round steak (1½ to 2 inches thick)
1   (1.25-ounce) package taco seasoning
Cooking spray
1   cup chopped onion
1   tablespoon white vinegar
1   (4.5-ounce) can chopped green chiles
1   (16-ounce) can fat-free refried beans
12  (8-inch) fat-free flour tortillas
1½  cups (6 ounces) shredded Monterey Jack cheese
1½  cups chopped plum tomato
¾   cup fat-free sour cream

**1.** Trim fat from steak; rub taco seasoning over both sides of steak. Place steak in an electric slow-cooker coated with cooking spray; add onion, vinegar, and green chiles. Cover with lid; cook on low-heat setting for 9 hours. Remove steak from slow-cooker, reserving cooking liquid; shred steak with 2 forks. Combine steak and reserved cooking liquid; stir well.

**2.** Warm beans and tortillas according to package

directions. Spread 2 tablespoons beans down center of each tortilla. Spoon a heaping ⅓ cup steak mixture over beans. Top each with 2 tablespoons cheese, 2 tablespoons tomato, and 1 tablespoon sour cream; roll up. Yield: 12 servings.

**POINTS:** 7; **Exchanges:** 2½ Med-fat Meat, 2 Starch
**Per serving:** CAL 350 (30% from fat); PRO 24g; FAT 11.8g (sat 6.1g); CARB 31.3g; FIB 3.3g; CHOL 49mg; IRON 4mg; SOD 839mg; CALC 175mg

## Mama's Chicken Stew

Make-Ahead Tip: Slow-cookers are the perfect solution for preparing dinner ahead of time. Cook the stew on the low-heat setting if you want it to simmer all day (about six to eight hours). Be sure to add the cornstarch mixture and green peas during the last 30 minutes of cooking so the cornstarch thickens properly and the peas do not overcook.

2   cups water
2   cups halved fresh mushrooms
1   cup frozen small white (pearl) onions
1   cup (½-inch-thick) sliced celery
1   cup thinly sliced carrot
1   teaspoon paprika
½   teaspoon salt
½   teaspoon rubbed sage
½   teaspoon dried thyme
½   teaspoon pepper
1   pound skinned, boned chicken breasts, cut
    into bite-size pieces
1   pound skinned, boned chicken thighs, cut
    into bite-size pieces
1   (14¼-ounce) can fat-free chicken broth
1   (6-ounce) can tomato paste
3   tablespoons cornstarch
¼   cup water
2   cups frozen green peas

**1.** Combine first 14 ingredients in a large electric slow-cooker. Cover with lid, and cook on high-heat setting for 4 hours or until carrot is tender. Combine cornstarch and water in a small bowl, and stir well. Add cornstarch mixture and peas to slow-cooker, and stir well. Cover and cook an additional 30 minutes. Yield: 8 servings (serving size: 1½ cups).

**POINTS:** 5; **Exchanges:** 3½ Very Lean Meat, 1½ Starch, 1 Veg
**Per serving:** CAL 257 (12% from fat); PRO 30.8g; FAT 3.5g (sat 0.8g); CARB 25.1g; FIB 2.8g; CHOL 78mg; IRON 3.2mg; SOD 359mg; CALC 83mg

## Smoke's Chili

Make-Ahead Tip: The chili may be made ahead and refrigerated up to four days in a nonaluminum container or frozen in an airtight container up to three months. Thaw if frozen, and then reheat over low heat.

2   teaspoons vegetable oil, divided
3½  pounds lean, boned chuck roast, cut into
    ½-inch pieces
3   cups chopped green bell pepper
1½  cups chopped onion
¼   to ½ teaspoon crushed red pepper
1   garlic clove, minced
2   tablespoons chili powder
1¼  teaspoons ground cumin
1   tablespoon brown sugar
1½  teaspoons dried oregano
½   teaspoon salt
1   (28-ounce) can whole tomatoes,
    undrained and chopped
1   (12-ounce) can tomato paste
1   (12-ounce) bottle beer
2   (15-ounce) cans kidney beans, drained
¾   cup low-fat sour cream
¾   cup (3 ounces) shredded reduced-fat
    Monterey Jack cheese

**1.** Heat ½ teaspoon oil in a large Dutch oven over medium-high heat. Add half of meat; cook 10 minutes or until browned. Remove meat from pan; drain in a colander. Repeat procedure with ½ teaspoon oil and remaining meat.

**2.** Heat remaining 1 teaspoon oil in pan over medium heat. Add bell pepper and next 3 ingredients, and sauté 8 minutes or until vegetables are tender. Add chili powder and cumin, and sauté 1 minute. Return meat to pan; add sugar and next 5 ingredients. Bring to a boil; cover, reduce heat, and simmer 45 minutes. Add beans; simmer, uncovered, an additional 40 minutes or until meat is tender. Serve with sour cream and shredded cheese. Yield: 12 servings (serving size: 1 cup chili, 1 tablespoon sour cream, and 1 tablespoon cheese).

**POINTS:** 7; **Exchanges:** 3½ Lean Meat, 1 Starch, 1 Veg, 1 Very Lean Meat
**Per serving:** CAL 330 (29% from fat); PRO 38.2g; FAT 10.8g (sat 4.3g); CARB 20g; FIB 3.4g; CHOL 94mg; IRON 5.5mg; SOD 527mg; CALC 133mg

Beer adds a depth of flavor to Pork-and-Squash Stew.

## Pork-and-Squash Stew

Make-Ahead Tip: You can prepare this stew ahead of time and store it in the refrigerator for up to four days in a nonaluminum container, or freeze it in an airtight container for up to three months. If frozen, thaw the stew and then reheat it over low heat.

1   pound pork shoulder
3   tablespoons all-purpose flour
4   teaspoons vegetable oil, divided
3   cups coarsely chopped onion
2¼  cups sliced carrot
½   teaspoon dried rosemary
½   teaspoon salt
¼   teaspoon pepper
1   (12-ounce) can beer
2   cups (¾-inch) peeled cubed butternut
     squash (about 1 pound)
2   teaspoons chopped fresh parsley

**1.** Trim fat from pork shoulder; cut pork into ¾-inch cubes, and set aside. Place flour in a large zip-top plastic bag. Add pork to bag; seal and shake to coat pork with flour mixture. Remove pork from bag; discard flour.

**2.** Heat 2 teaspoons oil in a large nonstick skillet over medium-high heat. Add pork, browning on all sides. Remove pork from skillet; set aside. Heat remaining 2 teaspoons oil in skillet. Add onion and carrot; sauté 5 minutes or until onion is tender.

**3.** Return pork to skillet; add rosemary, salt, pepper, and beer. Bring to a boil; cover, reduce heat, and simmer 30 minutes. Add squash; cover and simmer an additional 25 minutes or until squash is tender. Ladle stew into bowls, and sprinkle each serving with ½ teaspoon parsley. Yield: 4 servings (serving size: 2 cups).

*POINTS:* 7; **Exchanges:** 2½ Lean Meat, 2 Starch, 1 Fat, 1 Veg
**Per serving:** CAL 365 (34% from fat); PRO 25.7g; FAT 13.9g (sat 4g); CARB 35.5g; FIB 5.8g; CHOL 76mg; IRON 3mg; SOD 415mg; CALC 101mg

## Steak With Ale

Make-Ahead Tip: Marinate this steak while you work or sleep. When you're ready to cook, dinner is on the table in 10 minutes. Serve with Crispy Onion Rings, page 70.

1 (1½-pound) lean, boned top sirloin steak
½ cup finely chopped onion
½ cup boiling water
½ cup flat ale
1 tablespoon brown sugar
1 tablespoon red wine vinegar
1 teaspoon dried thyme
1 teaspoon beef-flavored bouillon granules
Cooking spray
Freshly ground pepper (optional)
Thyme sprigs (optional)

**1.** Trim fat from steak; set aside.

**2.** Place onion and next 6 ingredients in a blender; process until smooth. Pour ale mixture into a zip-top plastic bag, add steak. Seal and marinate in refrigerator 8 hours, turning bag occasionally.

**3.** Remove steak from bag; reserve marinade. Prepare grill. Place steak on grill rack coated with cooking spray; cover. Grill 5 minutes on each side or until desired degree of doneness, basting frequently with reserved marinade. Sprinkle with pepper and garnish with thyme before serving, if desired. Yield: 6 servings (serving size: 3 ounces).

POINTS: 4; Exchanges: 3½ Lean Meat
Per serving: CAL 177 (32% from fat); PRO 26g; FAT 6.3g (sat 2.4g); CARB 2.3g; FIB 0.2g; CHOL 76mg; IRON 3mg; SOD 110mg; CALC 14mg

## Ham-and-Lima Bean Casserole

Make-Ahead Tip: Assemble the casserole ahead, omitting biscuit topping. Cover; chill in refrigerator. Let stand at room temperature 30 minutes; add biscuit topping, and bake as directed.

1½ cups water
1½ cups frozen baby lima beans, thawed
¾ cup finely chopped green bell pepper
⅓ cup chopped onion
1¼ cups chopped extra-lean ham (about 6 ounces)
1 cup (4 ounces) shredded reduced-fat sharp cheddar cheese
1 teaspoon Worcestershire sauce
1 (14¾-ounce) can no-salt-added cream-style corn
Cooking spray

6 tablespoons skim milk
2 tablespoons chopped green onions
¾ cup low-fat biscuit and baking mix (such as Bisquick)

**1.** Preheat oven to 400°.

**2.** Bring water to a boil in a medium saucepan; add lima beans, bell pepper, and onion. Cover; cook 5 minutes, and drain. Combine lima bean mixture, ham, and next 3 ingredients; stir well. Spoon into a 2-quart casserole coated with cooking spray. Cover and bake at 400° for 20 minutes.

**3.** Combine milk and green onions; stir in baking mix. Drop batter onto ham mixture to form 6 biscuits. Bake at 400°, uncovered, 20 minutes, or until biscuits are golden. Yield: 6 servings (serving size: about ¾ cup casserole and 1 biscuit).

POINTS: 5; Exchanges: 2½ Starch, 1½ Lean Meat
Per serving: CAL 273 (22% from fat); PRO 17.8g; FAT 6.7g (sat 2.9g); CARB 36.5g; FIB 3.2g; CHOL 27mg; IRON 2.5mg; SOD 694mg; CALC 207mg

## Vegetable-and-Cheese Strata

1 teaspoon olive oil
2 cups diced zucchini
2 cups sliced fresh mushrooms
1 cup diced red bell pepper
1 cup diced onion
2 garlic cloves, crushed
¾ cup drained canned chopped artichoke hearts
8 cups (1-inch) cubed Italian bread (about 8 ounces)
Cooking spray
1 cup (4 ounces) shredded reduced-fat extra-sharp cheddar cheese
¼ cup (1 ounce) shredded fresh Parmesan cheese
1½ cups egg substitute
1 teaspoon dried Italian seasoning
½ teaspoon dry mustard
¼ teaspoon salt
¼ teaspoon pepper
1 (12-ounce) can evaporated skim milk
Oregano sprigs (optional)

**1.** Heat oil in a large nonstick skillet over medium-high heat. Add zucchini and next 4 ingredients; sauté 6 minutes or until tender. Remove from heat; stir in artichokes.

**2.** Arrange bread cubes in a 13- x 9-inch baking dish coated with cooking spray. Spoon zucchini mixture evenly over bread cubes; top with cheeses.

**3.** Combine egg substitute and next 5 ingredients in a bowl; stir with a whisk. Pour egg mixture over bread mixture. Cover with foil, and chill 8 hours.

**4.** Preheat oven to 325°.

**5.** Bake at 325°, covered, 1 hour or until bubbly. Garnish with oregano, if desired. Yield: 8 servings.

*POINTS:* 5; **Exchanges:** 1½ Starch, 1 Very Lean Meat, 1 Veg, ½ Med-fat Meat
**Per serving:** CAL 229 (19% from fat); PRO 17.5g; FAT 4.9g (sat 2.3g); CARB 29.1g; FIB 1.9g; CHOL 14mg; IRON 2.7mg; SOD 570mg; CALC 336mg

### Reuben Bake

Make-Ahead Tip: Assemble casserole up to eight hours ahead; cover and chill. Let stand at room temperature 30 minutes before baking.

5 cups peeled cubed baking potato
⅓ cup fat-free sour cream
¼ cup skim milk
½ teaspoon salt
¼ teaspoon pepper
Cooking spray
4 cups angel hair slaw
1 cup finely chopped lean deli corned beef (about ¼ pound)
½ teaspoon caraway seeds
¼ cup fat-free Thousand Island dressing
1¼ cups (5 ounces) shredded Swiss cheese, divided
Paprika

**1.** Preheat oven to 350°.

**2.** Place potato in a saucepan; cover with water, and bring to a boil. Cover, reduce heat, and simmer 20 minutes or until very tender; drain well.

**3.** Combine potato, sour cream, and next 3 ingredients; beat at medium speed of a mixer for 2 minutes or until smooth. Set aside.

**4.** Coat a nonstick skillet with cooking spray; place over medium heat until hot. Add cabbage, corned beef, and caraway seeds; sauté 4 minutes or until cabbage wilts. Remove from heat; stir in dressing.

**5.** Spread half of potato mixture in bottom of an 11- x 7-inch baking dish coated with cooking

spray; top with cabbage mixture, and sprinkle with 1 cup cheese. Spread remaining half of potato mixture over cheese; top with remaining ¼ cup cheese, and sprinkle with paprika. Bake at 350° for 40 minutes or until golden. Yield: 6 servings (serving size: 1⅓ cups).

*POINTS:* 5; **Exchanges:** 2 Starch, ½ Hi-fat Meat, ½ Lean Meat
**Per serving:** CAL 260 (31% from fat); PRO 11.2g; FAT 8.9g (sat 4.9g); CARB 30.7g; FIB 3.2g; CHOL 40mg; IRON 1.3mg; SOD 530mg; CALC 274mg

### Lentils With Garlic and Rosemary

Make-Ahead Tip: Not your typical slow-cooker recipe, this dish is ready in just three hours.

5 cups water
3 cups chopped onion
2 cups diced lean ham
1 cup diced carrot
1 teaspoon dried rosemary
¾ teaspoon rubbed sage
¼ teaspoon pepper
1 pound lentils
1 (14¼-ounce) can fat-free beef broth
2 garlic cloves, chopped
1 bay leaf
Chopped fresh parsley (optional)

**1.** Combine first 11 ingredients in an electric slow-cooker. Cover with lid, and cook on high-heat setting for 3 hours or until lentils are tender. Discard bay leaf. Garnish with parsley, if desired. Yield: 11 servings (serving size: 1 cup).

*POINTS:* 3; **Exchanges:** 2 Starch, 1½ Very Lean Meat
**Per serving:** CAL 196 (10% from fat); PRO 16.8g; FAT 2.2g (sat 0.7g); CARB 28.9g; FIB 6g; CHOL 13mg; IRON 4.1mg; SOD 248mg; CALC 38mg

### Chunky Vegetable Soup

Make-Ahead Tip: Make this soup ahead, and then refrigerate in an airtight container for up to one week, or freeze for up to three months.

Cooking spray
2 teaspoons vegetable oil
1 cup chopped onion
2 garlic cloves, minced
7 cups water
1 tablespoon dried basil
¾ teaspoon salt

½ teaspoon dried marjoram
½ teaspoon pepper
1 pound red potatoes, cut into 1-inch cubes
½ pound small carrots, cut into 1-inch pieces
1 (15-ounce) can cannellini beans or other white beans, drained
1 (14.5-ounce) can whole tomatoes, undrained and chopped
1 (10-ounce) package frozen large lima beans
½ cup uncooked orzo (rice-shaped pasta)
½ cup (2 ounces) shredded part-skim mozzarella cheese

**1.** Coat a large Dutch oven with cooking spray; add oil. Place over medium-high heat until hot. Add onion and garlic; sauté 5 minutes or until tender. Add water and next 9 ingredients; bring to a boil. Cover, reduce heat, and simmer 20 minutes. Add orzo, and cook, uncovered, over medium heat an additional 10 minutes or until orzo is tender. Ladle soup into individual bowls; sprinkle with mozzarella cheese. Yield: 8 servings (serving size: 1½ cups soup and 1 tablespoon cheese).

*POINTS:* 4; **Exchanges:** 2½ Starch, 1 Veg
**Per serving:** CAL 224 (12% from fat); PRO 10.6g; FAT 2.9g (sat 1g); CARB 40.4g; FIB 5.2g; CHOL 4mg; IRON 3.3mg; SOD 574mg; CALC 127mg

## Chicken Noodle Bake

1 cup 1% low-fat cottage cheese
½ cup tub-style light cream cheese
½ cup fat-free mayonnaise
½ cup fat-free sour cream
½ cup chopped onion
½ cup chopped green bell pepper
¼ cup minced fresh parsley
2 tablespoons stick margarine
⅓ cup all-purpose flour
½ cup skim milk
1 (10½-ounce) can low-salt chicken broth
½ teaspoon poultry seasoning
¼ teaspoon salt
¼ teaspoon pepper
Dash of garlic powder
6 cooked lasagna noodles, cooked without salt or fat
Cooking spray
3 cups diced cooked chicken breast, divided
½ cup dry breadcrumbs

2 tablespoons chopped fresh parsley
¼ teaspoon paprika

**1.** Preheat oven to 375°.

**2.** Combine first 4 ingredients; beat at high speed of a mixer until well blended. Stir in onion, bell pepper, and ¼ cup parsley, and set aside.

**3.** Melt margarine over medium heat in a medium saucepan. Add flour, and cook 1 minute, stirring constantly with a whisk. Gradually add skim milk and broth, stirring constantly. Bring to a boil over medium heat; cook 3 minutes or until mixture is thick, stirring constantly. Remove from heat; stir in poultry seasoning and next 3 ingredients.

**4.** Arrange 3 noodles in a 13- x 9-inch baking dish coated with cooking spray; top with half of cottage cheese mixture, half of chicken, and half of sauce. Repeat layers, ending with sauce.

**5.** Combine breadcrumbs, 2 tablespoons parsley, and paprika; sprinkle over casserole. Bake, uncovered, at 375° for 30 minutes. Serve immediately. Yield: 8 servings.

*POINTS:* 7; **Exchanges:** 3 Very Lean Meat, 2 Starch, 1½ Fat
**Per serving:** CAL 321 (24% from fat); PRO 26.1g; FAT 8.4g (sat 2.9g); CARB 33.2g; FIB 1.4g; CHOL 50mg; IRON 2.6mg; SOD 618mg; CALC 91mg

**Yielding 12 cups, Chunky Vegetable Soup makes enough for future meals.**

# One Size Does Not Fit All

WHEN IT'S JUST THE TWO OF YOU, THESE RECIPES ARE A PERFECT FIT.

G*etting a healthful meal on the table at a decent hour is challenge enough. The last thing you need to be doing during the dinner hour is scaling back a recipe designed to feed eight when it's just the two of you. Whether "the two of you" means you and a child because your spouse is working late, you and your husband because the kids have plans of their own, or you're going solo, but want leftovers to pack for lunch, this chapter is full of ideas. There's Vegetarian Pizzas, Lemon-Chicken Pasta, and Pork Fried Rice for casual weeknights, and Glazed Cornish Hen and Grilled Tuna With Herbed Mayonnaise for those nights when your table for two will be set with a tablecloth and candles. Math skills, after all, shouldn't be a prerequisite for cooking dinner.*

**Linguine With Mussels is quick, economical, and worthy of candlelight.**

## Linguine With Mussels

2 teaspoons olive oil
½ cup chopped fennel bulb
½ cup finely chopped onion
2 garlic cloves, minced
1 cup diced tomato
1 cup dry vermouth
3 tablespoons chopped fresh parsley
1 tablespoon tomato paste
1 teaspoon chopped fresh thyme
¼ teaspoon salt
⅛ teaspoon ground red pepper
28 mussels, scrubbed and debearded
2 teaspoons cornstarch
2 tablespoons water
2 cups hot cooked linguine, cooked without salt or fat (about 4 ounces uncooked pasta)

**1.** Heat oil in a large nonstick skillet over medium heat. Add fennel, onion, and garlic; sauté 5 minutes. Add tomato and next 6 ingredients; bring to a boil. Add mussels; cover and cook 3 minutes or until shells open. Remove from heat; discard any unopened shells. Let mussels cool slightly. Reserve 10 shells with meat intact. Remove meat from remaining shells, and add meat to tomato mixture; discard shells.

**2.** Combine cornstarch and water; stir well. Add cornstarch mixture to tomato mixture; bring to a boil over medium heat, and cook 2 minutes, stirring constantly. Spoon 1 cup pasta onto each of 2 serving plates; top each with 1 cup sauce and 5 mussels in shells. Yield: 2 servings.

*POINTS:* 7; **Exchanges:** 4 Starch, 1 Fat, ½ Very Lean Meat
**Per serving:** CAL 376 (17% from fat); PRO 16.3g; FAT 7.3g (sat 1.1g); CARB 61.2g; FIB 5.1g; CHOL 16mg; IRON 6.5mg; SOD 489mg; CALC 90mg

## Glazed Cornish Hen

1 (1½-pound) Cornish hen
3 tablespoons low-sugar apricot spread
2 teaspoons lime juice
2 teaspoons low-salt soy sauce
⅛ teaspoon ground cinnamon

**1.** Preheat oven to 350°.

**2.** Remove and discard giblets and neck from hen. Rinse hen under cold water, and pat dry. Remove skin, and trim fat. Split hen in half lengthwise. Place hen halves, meaty sides up, on a broiler pan. Bake at 350° for 30 minutes.

**3.** Combine apricot spread and next 3 ingredients in a small saucepan; cook over low heat until spread melts. Remove 2 tablespoons apricot mixture, and brush over hen halves. Bake an additional 30 minutes or until juices run clear. Spoon remaining apricot mixture evenly over hen halves. Yield: 2 servings (serving size: 1 hen half).

*POINTS:* 6; **Exchanges:** 3 Lean Meat, 1½ Very Lean Meat, ½ Starch
**Per serving:** CAL 257 (29% from fat); PRO 33.1g; FAT 8.4g (sat 2g); CARB 10.1g; FIB 0g; CHOL 101mg; IRON 1.5mg; SOD 298mg; CALC 20mg

## Catfish-and-Slaw Sandwiches

1 cup thinly sliced green cabbage
3 tablespoons minced radish
1 tablespoon plain fat-free yogurt
1 tablespoon light mayonnaise
½ teaspoon paprika
¼ teaspoon garlic powder
¼ teaspoon pepper
2 (4-ounce) farm-raised catfish fillets
Cooking spray
2 (2-ounce) Kaiser rolls
6 (¼-inch thick) slices tomato

**1.** Combine first 4 ingredients in a bowl; stir well, and set aside. Combine paprika, garlic powder, and pepper; sprinkle over fillets. Coat a large nonstick skillet with cooking spray; place over medium-high heat until hot. Add fillets; cook 4 minutes on each side or until fish flakes easily when tested with a fork. Divide cabbage mixture evenly between roll bottoms; top with fillets, tomato slices, and roll tops. Yield: 2 servings.

*POINTS:* 7; **Exchanges:** 2½ Starch, 3 Very Lean Meat
**Per serving:** CAL 353 (27% from fat); PRO 27.7g; FAT 10.5g (sat 2.2g); CARB 35.8g; FIB 2.5g; CHOL 68mg; IRON 4.1mg; SOD 516mg; CALC 123mg

## Pasta With Sausage and Vegetables

Cooking spray
4 ounces turkey Italian sausage, cut diagonally into ¼-inch-thick slices
1 cup slivered onion
1 cup seeded chopped tomato

1 garlic clove, minced

1½ teaspoons all-purpose flour

½ cup water

⅛ teaspoon salt

⅛ teaspoon pepper

½ cup fresh broccoli florets

½ cup (2- x ¼-inch) julienne-cut red bell pepper

½ cup (2- x ¼-inch) julienne-cut yellow bell pepper

1 cup hot cooked penne, cooked without salt or fat (about 4 ounces uncooked tubular pasta)

2 teaspoons minced fresh basil

**1.** Coat a large nonstick skillet with cooking spray; place over medium-high heat until hot.

Add sausage; cook 5 minutes or until browned, stirring frequently. Remove from skillet; set aside, and keep warm. Wipe drippings from skillet with a paper towel.

**2.** Recoat skillet with cooking spray, and place over medium-high heat until hot. Add onion; sauté 3 minutes. Add tomato and garlic; sauté 5 minutes. Stir in flour. Gradually add water, salt, and pepper, stirring constantly. Bring to a boil; cover, reduce heat, and simmer 10 minutes, stirring frequently. Add broccoli and bell peppers; cook 10 minutes or until vegetables are tender and sauce is thick, stirring occasionally. Stir in

**For a little Cajun flair, try Catfish-and-Slaw Sandwiches.**

**Flour tortillas provide a simple, crunchy crust for Vegetarian Pizzas.**

onion and garlic; sauté 1 minute. Add mushrooms and carrot; sauté 2 minutes. Remove from heat; stir in cilantro.

**2.** Place tortillas on a baking sheet; broil 2 minutes. Turn tortillas over; broil an additional 1 minute or until crisp.

**3.** Remove from oven; top each tortilla with ¼ cup cheese, ¼ cup beans, and half of mushroom mixture. Sprinkle remaining cheese evenly over pizzas; broil 1 minute or until cheese melts. Yield: 2 servings.

POINTS: 5; **Exchanges:** 2½ Starch, 1½ Med-fat Meat
**Per serving:** CAL 296 (29% from fat); PRO 17g; FAT 9.7g (sat 4.7g); CARB 37.6g; FIB 6.4g; CHOL 25mg; IRON 2.2mg; SOD 436mg; CALC 334mg

## Onion, Bacon, and Spinach Frittata

2   turkey-bacon slices, chopped
⅛   teaspoon pepper
⅛   teaspoon ground nutmeg
5   large egg whites
1   large egg
1½  cups thinly sliced Vidalia or other sweet onion, separated into rings
2   tablespoons water
¼   teaspoon sugar
4   cups torn fresh spinach
¼   cup (1 ounce) shredded part-skim mozzarella cheese

**1.** Preheat oven to 450°.

**2.** Cook turkey-bacon in a large nonstick skillet over medium heat until crisp. Combine bacon and next 4 ingredients in a large bowl; stir well, and set aside.

**3.** Add onion to skillet; cover and cook over medium heat 5 minutes or until crisp-tender, stirring occasionally. Add water and sugar; sauté 5 minutes or until onion is tender and golden brown. Add spinach; cover and cook 2 minutes or until spinach wilts. Stir in egg mixture; spread evenly in bottom of skillet. Cook over medium-low heat 5 minutes or until almost set.

**4.** Wrap handle of skillet with foil; place skillet in oven, and bake at 450° for 5 minutes or until

sausage and pasta; sprinkle with basil. Yield: 2 servings (serving size: 1¼ cups).

POINTS: 10; **Exchanges:** 4 Starch, 3 Veg, 1 Hi-fat Meat, 1 Fat
**Per serving:** CAL 539 (29% from fat); PRO 24g; FAT 17.6g (sat 6.6g); CARB 71g; FIB 9.8g; CHOL 75mg; IRON 4.9mg; SOD 630mg; CALC 77mg

## Vegetarian Pizzas

Cooking spray
3   tablespoons chopped red onion
1   garlic clove, minced
½   cup sliced fresh mushrooms
⅓   cup shredded carrot
1   tablespoon minced fresh cilantro
2   (6-inch) flour tortillas
¾   cup (3 ounces) shredded part-skim mozzarella cheese, divided
½   cup drained canned kidney beans

**1.** Coat a medium nonstick skillet with cooking spray; place over medium heat until hot. Add

set. Sprinkle with mozzarella cheese, and bake an additional 1 minute or until cheese melts. Yield: 2 servings.

**Note:** Substitute 1 cup egg substitute for egg whites and egg, if desired.

*POINTS:* 4; **Exchanges:** 2 Veg, 1½ Very Lean Meat, 1 Hi-fat Meat
**Per serving:** CAL 205 (33% from fat); PRO 21.2g; FAT 7.5g (sat 2.9g); CARB 13.6g; FIB 6.1g; CHOL 127mg; IRON 3.6mg; SOD 659mg; CALC 238mg

## Shrimp-and-Mango Salad

Although this recipe calls for large shrimp (there are fewer to peel), medium-size shrimp can also be used.

¼ cup light mayonnaise
2 tablespoons prepared horseradish
1 tablespoon white vinegar
⅛ teaspoon pepper
¾ pound large shrimp, cooked and peeled
1 cup peeled cubed mango
¾ cup hot cooked rice, cooked without salt or fat
¼ cup chopped red bell pepper
¼ cup chopped green bell pepper

**1.** Combine first 4 ingredients in a large bowl, and stir well. Add shrimp and remaining ingredients, and toss gently to coat. Yield: 2 servings (serving size: 1½ cups).

*POINTS:* 7; **Exchanges:** 3½ Very Lean Meat, 1½ Starch, 1 Fruit, 1 Fat
**Per serving:** CAL 351 (21% from fat); PRO 29.1g; FAT 8g (sat 2.5g); CARB 40.2g; FIB 2.3g; CHOL 249mg; IRON 5.4mg; SOD 629mg; CALC 83mg

## Marinated Lamb Chops With Herbs

4 (3-ounce) lean lamb rib chops
¼ cup dry red wine
2 tablespoons chopped fresh or ½ teaspoon dried mint
2 tablespoons low-salt soy sauce
1½ teaspoons chopped fresh or ¼ teaspoon dried rosemary
½ teaspoon coarsely ground pepper
1 garlic clove, crushed
Rosemary sprigs (optional)

**1.** Trim fat from chops. Combine chops, wine, and next 5 ingredients in a large zip-top plastic bag; seal bag, and marinate in refrigerator 8 hours, turning bag occasionally. Remove chops from bag, reserving marinade.

**2.** Prepare grill or broiler. Place chops on grill rack or broiler pan; cook 4 minutes on each side or until desired degree of doneness, basting frequently with reserved marinade. Garnish with rosemary sprigs, if desired. Yield: 2 servings (serving size: 2 chops).

*POINTS:* 7; **Exchanges:** 4 Med-fat Meat
**Per serving:** CAL 301 (45% from fat); PRO 32.5g; FAT 14.9g (sat 5.3g); CARB 2.7g; FIB 0.3g; CHOL 103mg; IRON 3.5mg; SOD 584mg; CALC 39mg

## Cool Chicken Salad Shells

6 uncooked jumbo pasta shells (not macaroni)
3 tablespoons light mayonnaise
2 tablespoons fat-free Italian dressing
¼ teaspoon onion powder
1 cup chopped cooked chicken breast (about 6 ounces)
⅔ cup drained canned chopped artichoke hearts
¼ cup finely chopped red bell pepper
2 tablespoons chopped ripe olives
6 fresh basil leaves

**1.** Cook pasta shells in boiling water 10 minutes. Drain and rinse under cold water. Drain well, and set aside.

**2.** Combine mayonnaise, Italian dressing, and onion powder in a medium bowl; stir well. Add chicken, artichokes, bell pepper, and olives; stir

**Serve Marinated Lamb Chops With Herbs alongside baby carrots and a couscous pilaf.**

Lemon-Chicken Pasta

well. Line each shell with a basil leaf; stuff with about 3 tablespoons chicken mixture. Serve at room temperature or chilled. Yield: 2 servings (serving size: 3 stuffed shells).

POINTS: 8; Exchanges: 3½ Very Lean Meat, 2 Starch, 2 Fat, 1 Veg
Per serving: CAL 306 (25% from fat); PRO 24.5g; FAT 8.4g (sat 2.3g); CARB 31.1g; FIB 2.7g; CHOL 81mg; IRON 3.1mg; SOD 624mg; CALC 62mg

## Lemon-Chicken Pasta

Cooking spray
1 teaspoon olive oil
2 garlic cloves, minced
6 ounces skinned, boned chicken breast, cut into ¼-inch-wide strips
½ cup frozen green peas, thawed
⅓ cup shredded carrot
½ cup low-salt chicken broth
2 tablespoons tub-style light cream cheese
2 cups hot cooked farfalle, cooked without salt or fat (about 1¼ cups uncooked bow tie pasta)
3 tablespoons grated Parmesan cheese
½ teaspoon grated lemon rind
⅛ teaspoon salt
⅛ teaspoon pepper
Fresh chives (optional)

1. Coat a large nonstick skillet with cooking spray; add oil, and place over medium-high heat until hot. Add garlic; sauté 15 seconds. Add chicken; sauté 1 minute. Add peas and carrot; sauté 1 minute. Remove chicken mixture from skillet; set aside.
2. Add chicken broth and cream cheese to skillet, and cook over medium-high heat 3 minutes or until cream cheese melts, stirring constantly with a whisk. Return chicken mixture to skillet. Stir in pasta, Parmesan cheese, lemon rind, salt, and pepper; cook 1 minute. Garnish with fresh chives, if desired. Yield: 2 servings (serving size: 1½ cups).

POINTS: 8; Exchanges: 3½ Very Lean Meat, 3 Starch, 1½ Fat
Per serving: CAL 422 (21% from fat); PRO 33.6g; FAT 9.7g (sat 3.6g); CARB 48.4g; FIB 4.6g; CHOL 63mg; IRON 3.7mg; SOD 478mg; CALC 163mg

## Grilled Tuna With Herbed Mayonnaise

If you believe folklore, this low-fat mayonnaise has all kinds of healthful benefits. The oregano supposedly helps end toothaches, baldness, and aching muscles, while the tarragon allegedly prevents fatigue.

¼ cup fat-free mayonnaise
¼ cup plain fat-free yogurt
1 teaspoon chopped fresh oregano
1 teaspoon chopped fresh tarragon
1 teaspoon lemon juice
¼ teaspoon salt
¼ teaspoon pepper
4 (6-ounce) tuna steaks (about 1 inch thick)
Cooking spray

1. Combine first 5 ingredients in a small bowl; stir well, and set aside. Sprinkle salt and pepper over tuna.
2. Prepare grill. Place tuna on grill rack coated with cooking spray; grill 3 minutes on each side or until tuna is medium-rare or desired degree of doneness. Serve with mayonnaise mixture. Yield: 2 servings (serving size: 1 tuna steak and 2 tablespoons mayonnaise mixture).

POINTS: 6; Exchanges: 6 Very Lean Meat, ½ Starch
Per serving: CAL 267 (29% from fat); PRO 40.5g; FAT 8.5g (sat 2.2g); CARB 4.6g; FIB 0.1g; CHOL 65mg; IRON 1.9mg; SOD 414mg; CALC 33mg

## Lamb Chops Marsala

4 (4-ounce) lean lamb loin chops
Cooking spray
½ cup water
½ cup dry Marsala
2 tablespoons tomato paste
1 cup sliced fresh mushrooms
¼ cup chopped onion

1. Trim fat from chops. Coat a large nonstick skillet with cooking spray; place over medium-high heat until hot. Add chops; cook 4 minutes on each side or until desired degree of doneness. Remove chops from skillet; set aside, and keep warm. Wipe drippings from skillet with a paper towel.
2. Combine water, wine, and tomato paste in a bowl; stir with a whisk until mixture is blended. Add wine mixture, mushrooms, and onion to

skillet, and cook over high heat 2 minutes or until thick, stirring constantly. Spoon sauce over chops. Yield: 2 servings (serving size: 2 chops and about ⅓ cup sauce).

*POINTS:* 5; **Exchanges:** 4 Lean Meat, 1 Veg
**Per serving:** CAL 248 (30% from fat); PRO 32.9g; FAT 8.4g (sat 3g); CARB 8.6g; FIB 1.6g; CHOL 111mg; IRON 3.3mg; SOD 95mg; CALC 29mg

## Turkey Waldorf Salad With Yogurt Dressing

1    cup chopped cooked turkey breast
1    cup diced Red Delicious apple
½    cup chopped celery
2    tablespoons chopped walnuts
2    tablespoons raisins
½    cup plain low-fat yogurt
1    tablespoon honey
1    teaspoon grated orange rind
4    curly leaf lettuce leaves

**1.** Combine first 5 ingredients in a medium bowl. Combine yogurt, honey, and orange rind; stir well. Pour yogurt mixture over turkey mixture; toss gently to coat.

**2.** Spoon salad mixture evenly onto lettuce-lined plates. Serve immediately. Yield: 2 servings.

*POINTS:* 6; **Exchanges:** 3 Very Lean Meat, 1½ Fruit, 1 Veg, 1 Fat, ½ Starch
**Per serving:** CAL 306 (21% from fat); PRO 26.2g; FAT 7g (sat 1.1g); CARB 36.7g; FIB 3.8g; CHOL 47mg; IRON 1.8mg; SOD 122mg; CALC 142mg

## Oyster Bisque

1    tablespoon all-purpose flour
¾    cup evaporated skim milk
1    teaspoon olive oil
¼    cup finely chopped carrot
¼    cup finely chopped celery
¼    cup finely chopped red bell pepper
1    (12-ounce) container standard oysters, drained
2    teaspoons chili sauce
1    teaspoon Worcestershire sauce
Dash of ground red pepper
¼    teaspoon paprika

**1.** Place flour in a small bowl; gradually add milk, stirring with a whisk until blended. Set aside.

**2.** Heat oil in a medium saucepan over medium-high heat. Add carrot, celery, and bell pepper; sauté 5 minutes or until tender. Add flour mixture; reduce heat to medium, and cook 3 minutes or until thick and bubbly, stirring constantly. Add oysters; cook 2 minutes or until edges of oysters curl. Remove from heat; stir in chili sauce, Worcestershire sauce, and red pepper. Ladle soup into bowls; sprinkle with paprika. Yield: 2 servings (serving size: 1 cup).

*POINTS:* 5; **Exchanges:** 1 Sk Milk, 1½ Lean Meat, ½ Fat, ½ Starch
**Per serving:** CAL 218 (25% from fat); PRO 17.7g; FAT 6g (sat 1.3g); CARB 22.7g; FIB 1.2g; CHOL 78mg; IRON 10mg; SOD 334mg; CALC 354mg

## Open-Faced Vegetable Melt

This meatless sandwich resembles a Frenchbread pizza.

½    teaspoon olive oil
¼    cup thinly sliced onion
½    small zucchini, halved lengthwise and sliced (about ½ cup)
1    garlic clove, minced
½    cup seeded coarsely chopped tomato
¼    cup chopped bottled roasted red bell peppers
¼    teaspoon dried thyme
⅛    teaspoon pepper
½    cup (2 ounces) shredded provolone cheese, divided
1    (5-inch) piece unsliced Italian bread (about ¼ pound), cut in half horizontally and toasted
1    tablespoon grated Parmesan cheese

**1.** Heat oil in a medium nonstick skillet over medium heat. Add onion, zucchini, and garlic; sauté 5 minutes or until tender. Add tomato and next 3 ingredients; sauté 1 minute.

**2.** Sprinkle 2 tablespoons provolone cheese over each piece of bread; top with vegetable mixture. Sprinkle remaining ¼ cup provolone cheese and Parmesan cheese evenly over sandwiches. Broil 2 minutes or until cheese melts. Serve immediately. Yield: 2 servings.

*POINTS:* 6; **Exchanges:** 2 Starch, 2 Veg, 1 Hi-fat Meat
**Per serving:** CAL 307 (30% from fat); PRO 14.7g; FAT 10.2g (sat 5.5g); CARB 39.2g; FIB 3.1g; CHOL 22mg; IRON 2.3mg; SOD 731mg; CALC 278mg

## Beef, Pepper, and Shiitake Mushroom Stir-fry

Cooking spray
1   teaspoon olive oil, divided
1   (6-ounce) filet mignon steak, cut into
    ½-inch strips
½   cup sliced shallots
½   cup (¼-inch-thick) strips green bell pepper
½   cup (¼-inch-thick) strips red bell pepper
½   cup (¼-inch-thick) strips yellow bell
    pepper
3   garlic cloves, minced
2   cups sliced fresh shiitake mushroom caps
    (about 1 [3½-ounce] package)
¼   cup dry white wine
½   cup fat-free beef broth
1   tablespoon chopped fresh basil
¼   teaspoon salt
¼   teaspoon pepper
1½  cups hot cooked rice, cooked without
    salt or fat

**1.** Coat a large nonstick skillet with cooking spray; add ½ teaspoon oil, and place over medium-high heat until hot. Add beef; stir-fry 2 minutes. Remove beef from skillet; set aside. Wipe drippings from skillet with a paper towel.

**2.** Heat remaining ½ teaspoon oil in skillet over medium-high heat. Add shallots, bell pepper strips, and garlic; stir-fry 1 minute. Add mushrooms; stir-fry 2 minutes. Stir in wine; cook 1 minute. Add broth; reduce heat, and simmer 3 minutes. Return beef to skillet, and cook 1 minute. Remove from heat; stir in basil, salt, and pepper. Serve over rice. Yield: 2 servings (serving size: 1 cup beef mixture and ¾ cup rice).

*POINTS*: 8; **Exchanges:** 3½ Starch, 1½ Lean Meat, 1 Veg, ½ Fat
**Per serving:** CAL 406 (20% from fat); PRO 24.7g; FAT 9.2g (sat 2.7g); CARB 55.8g; FIB 4g; CHOL 53mg; IRON 6.8mg; SOD 355mg; CALC 60mg

Beef, Pepper, and Shiitake Mushroom Stir-fry is a satisfying one-dish meal.

eggs from skillet with a slotted spoon. Spoon half of tomato mixture onto each of 2 plates; top with eggs. Sprinkle each with 1 tablespoon cheese and 1 tablespoon green onions. Yield: 2 servings.

*POINTS:* 5; **Exchanges:** 2½ Starch, 1½ Med-fat Meat, 1 Veg, 1 Very Lean Meat
**Per serving:** CAL 337 (19% from fat); PRO 23.1g; FAT 7.1g (sat 2.5g); CARB 45.7g; FIB 13.9g; CHOL 226mg; IRON 5.6mg; SOD 551mg; CALC 272mg

## Pork Fried Rice

Five-spice powder, available in most supermarkets, is a mixture of cinnamon, cloves, fennel seeds, peppercorns, and star anise.

1    (6-ounce) pork tenderloin
⅛    teaspoon five-spice powder
Cooking spray
1½  teaspoons vegetable oil, divided
½    teaspoon fennel seeds, crushed
½    cup chopped fresh broccoli florets
½    cup sliced fresh mushrooms
¼    cup chopped green onions
¼    cup shredded carrot
1½  cups hot cooked rice, cooked without
      salt or fat
1    tablespoon low-salt soy sauce
⅛    teaspoon pepper

**1.** Trim fat from pork; cut pork into ¼-inch cubes. Combine pork and five-spice powder; toss to coat. Coat a large nonstick skillet with cooking spray; place over medium-high heat until hot. Add pork; stir-fry 3 minutes or until browned. Spoon pork into a medium bowl; set aside.

**2.** Heat ¾ teaspoon oil in skillet over medium-high heat. Add fennel seeds; stir-fry 30 seconds. Add broccoli and next 3 ingredients; stir-fry 3 minutes. Add vegetable mixture to pork mixture, and set aside. Heat remaining ¾ teaspoon oil in skillet over medium heat. Add rice; stir-fry 2 minutes. Stir in soy sauce and pepper. Return pork-vegetable mixture to skillet; stir-fry until thoroughly heated. Yield: 2 servings (serving size: 1½ cups).

*POINTS:* 6; **Exchanges:** 3 Starch, 2 Very Lean Meat, ½ Fat
**Per serving:** CAL 322 (18% from fat); PRO 22.8g; FAT 6.3g (sat 1.4g); CARB 42.5g; FIB 2.6g; CHOL 55mg; IRON 3.4mg; SOD 298mg; CALC 55mg

**The secret to Quick Rosemary Steaks is simmering the beef in pear nectar.**

## Huevos Rancheros

1    (14.5-ounce) can no-salt-added whole
      tomatoes, undrained and chopped
1    (15-ounce) can no-salt-added black beans,
      drained
1    (4.5-ounce) can chopped green chiles
2    tablespoons chopped fresh cilantro
2    teaspoons chili powder
½    teaspoon ground cumin
¼    teaspoon salt
⅛    teaspoon pepper
2    large eggs
2    tablespoons (½ ounce) shredded reduced-
      fat sharp cheddar cheese
2    tablespoons chopped green onions

**1.** Combine first 8 ingredients in a large nonstick skillet; bring to a boil. Cover, reduce heat, and simmer 10 minutes, stirring occasionally.

**2.** Break each egg into a custard cup, and slip eggs from cups into tomato mixture. Cover and simmer 6 minutes or until eggs are done. Remove

## Quick Rosemary Steaks

2   (4-ounce) filet mignon steaks (1 inch thick)
Cooking spray
¼   teaspoon olive oil
¼   cup pear nectar
¾   teaspoon all-purpose flour
¼   teaspoon dried rosemary, crushed
⅛   teaspoon salt
⅓   cup evaporated skim milk
1   teaspoon white wine vinegar
1   medium red or green Bartlett pear, sliced
Rosemary sprigs (optional)

**1.** Trim fat from steaks. Coat a medium nonstick skillet with cooking spray; add olive oil, and place over medium-high heat until hot. Add steaks; cook 1 minute on each side or until browned. Reduce heat to low, and add pear nectar. Cover and simmer 10 minutes or until steaks are done. Remove steaks from skillet; set aside, and keep warm.

**2.** Combine flour, rosemary, and salt in a bowl. Gradually add milk and vinegar, stirring with a whisk until blended; add to skillet. Bring to a boil; cook 30 seconds or until thick, stirring constantly. Spoon sauce on individual serving plates; place steaks on top of sauce. Arrange pear slices around steak. Garnish with rosemary sprigs, if desired. Yield: 2 servings.

*POINTS:* 6; **Exchanges:** 3½ Lean Meat, 1½ Fruit
**Per serving:** CAL 282 (28% from fat); PRO 27.4g; FAT 8.8g (sat 3.1g); CARB 23g; FIB 2.3g; CHOL 72mg; IRON 3.6mg; SOD 258mg; CALC 143mg

## Spinach-and-Goat Cheese French Bread Pizzas

Cooking spray
2   cups torn fresh spinach
⅛   teaspoon pepper
1   (7-inch-long) French roll (about 3½ ounces)
¼   cup tomato paste
¼   teaspoon dried Italian seasoning
½   garlic clove, minced
1   hard-cooked large egg, sliced
2   tablespoons (½ ounce) crumbled goat cheese

**1.** Coat a large nonstick skillet with cooking spray, and place over low heat until hot. Add spinach; cover and cook 7 minutes or until spinach wilts, stirring occasionally. Sprinkle with pepper, and set aside.

**2.** Cut roll in half horizontally, and place, cut sides up, on a baking sheet. Broil 2 minutes or until golden.

**3.** Combine tomato paste, Italian seasoning, and garlic in a small bowl; stir well, and spread over cut sides of bread. Top with spinach mixture, egg, and cheese. Broil 2 minutes or until cheese melts. Yield: 2 servings.

**Note:** For a more pungent flavor, substitute blue cheese for the goat cheese.

*POINTS:* 4; **Exchanges:** 2 Starch, 1 Med-fat Meat
**Per serving:** CAL 231 (27% from fat); PRO 11.7g; FAT 6.9g (sat 3.3g); CARB 31.1g; FIB 4.6g; CHOL 124mg; IRON 4.1mg; SOD 483mg; CALC 174mg

## Crab Risotto

Serve this dish immediately as you would any risotto.

2   cups low-salt chicken broth
¾   cup water
1   teaspoon olive oil
3   tablespoons finely chopped onion
¾   cup uncooked Arborio rice or other short-grain rice
3   tablespoons dry white wine

**For a light meal, try Spinach-and-Goat Cheese French Bread Pizzas with a simple salad of yellow tomatoes and green beans.**

**Pair Roast Beef-and-Blue Cheese Sandwiches with your favorite soup and slaw.**

½ pound lump crabmeat, shell pieces removed and drained
3 tablespoons minced fresh parsley
½ teaspoon dried basil
2 tablespoons grated Parmesan cheese

**1.** Bring broth and water to a simmer in a small saucepan (do not boil). Keep warm over low heat.

**2.** Heat oil in a medium saucepan over medium-high heat. Add onion; sauté 2 minutes. Add rice; reduce heat to medium, and cook 3 minutes, stirring constantly. Stir in wine; cook until the liquid is nearly absorbed, stirring constantly. Add broth mixture, ½ cup at a time, stirring constantly; cook until each portion of broth is absorbed before adding the next (about 20 minutes). Stir in crabmeat, parsley, and basil; cook 2 minutes or until thoroughly heated, stirring constantly.

Spoon into shallow bowls; sprinkle with cheese. Yield: 2 servings (serving size: 1½ cups risotto and 1 tablespoon cheese).

*POINTS:* 9; **Exchanges:** 4 Starch, 2½ Very Lean Meat, 1 Fat
**Per serving:** CAL 453 (15% from fat); PRO 29.7g; FAT 7.5g (sat 2.6g); CARB 64g; FIB 1.6g; CHOL 103mg; IRON 5.8mg; SOD 452mg; CALC 193mg

## Roast Beef-and-Blue Cheese Sandwiches

Have the deli thinly slice or even shave the roast beef to create a taller sandwich.

2 tablespoons fat-free mayonnaise
1 tablespoon Dijon mustard
¼ teaspoon pepper
2 (2-ounce) onion sandwich buns, split
2 romaine lettuce leaves
4 (¼-inch-thick) slices tomato
4 green bell pepper rings

4   (¼-inch-thick) slices red onion
4   ounces thinly sliced lean deli roast beef
2   tablespoons (½ ounce) crumbled blue
    cheese

**1.** Combine first 3 ingredients in a bowl; stir well. Spread evenly over cut sides of buns. Arrange lettuce leaves and next 4 ingredients over bottom halves of buns; top with cheese and top halves of buns. Yield: 2 servings.

*POINTS:* 7; **Exchanges:** 2 Starch, 1½ Med-fat Meat, 1 Veg
**Per serving:** CAL 309 (31% from fat); PRO 18.6g; FAT 10.7g (sat 4.5g); CARB 35.1g; FIB 2.5g; CHOL 5mg; IRON 2mg; SOD 1,133mg; CALC 53mg

## Chili-Lime Shrimp Kabobs

20  large shrimp (about 12 ounces)
2   tablespoons minced fresh cilantro
1   tablespoon seeded minced jalapeño pepper
2   tablespoons fresh lime juice
1   teaspoon dried oregano
1   teaspoon chili powder
1   teaspoon olive oil
½   teaspoon salt
½   teaspoon pepper
1   garlic clove, minced
8   cherry tomatoes
Cooking spray
2   cups hot cooked rice, cooked without salt
    or fat

**1.** Peel shrimp, leaving tails intact.

**2.** Combine cilantro and next 8 ingredients in a large zip-top plastic bag; add shrimp and tomatoes. Seal bag, and marinate in refrigerator for 1 hour, turning bag occasionally. Remove shrimp and tomatoes from bag, reserving marinade.

**3.** Thread shrimp and tomatoes alternately onto each of 4 (10-inch) skewers. Prepare grill or broiler. Place kabobs on grill rack or broiler pan coated with cooking spray; cook 6 minutes or until done, turning and basting occasionally with reserved marinade. Serve kabobs over rice. Yield: 2 servings.

*POINTS:* 9; **Exchanges:** 3½ Starch, 4 Very Lean Meat, 1 Veg, ½ Fat
**Per serving:** CAL 455 (12% from fat); PRO 39.8g; FAT 6.3g (sat 1g); CARB 57.8g; FIB 2.7g; CHOL 259mg; IRON 7.1mg; SOD 859mg; CALC 140mg

## Citrus-Glazed Pork

1   (8-ounce) pork tenderloin
¼   teaspoon coarsely ground pepper
⅓   cup orange marmalade
2   tablespoons chopped fresh mint
2   tablespoons low-salt soy sauce
2   garlic cloves, minced
Cooking spray
Mint sprigs (optional)

**1.** Trim fat from pork. Cut pork horizontally into 2 (4-ounce) pieces. Cut a lengthwise slit down the center of each piece of tenderloin two-thirds of the way through the meat. Sprinkle with coarsely ground pepper.

**2.** Combine marmalade and next 3 ingredients in a small bowl, and stir well. Brush marmalade mixture evenly over pork, reserving remaining marmalade mixture.

**3.** Prepare grill. Place pork on grill rack coated with cooking spray; grill 8 minutes on each side or until instant read thermometer registers 160° (slightly pink), basting frequently with reserved marmalade mixture. Garnish with mint sprigs, if desired. Yield: 2 servings (serving size: 3 ounces).

*POINTS:* 6; **Exchanges:** 2½ Starch, 2½ Very Lean Meat
**Per serving:** CAL 291 (15% from fat); PRO 26.2g; FAT 4.7g (sat 1.5g); CARB 36.2g; FIB 0.1g; CHOL 83mg; IRON 1.6mg; SOD 480mg; CALC 36mg

A perfect patio meal: Citrus-Glazed Pork, orzo, and sweet broiled pineapple

# Guess Who's Coming to Dinner

WE'VE CREATED 21 MENUS TO TAKE THE
HASSLE OUT OF BEING THE HOST.

*I*t's hard to imagine that anything good came out of the Great Depression, but even that huge cloud had a proverbial silver lining. The Depression changed the way Americans entertained. Suddenly maidless, hostesses found themselves responsible for planning and cooking meals. The stock market crash hit everyone hard, but those who could opened their homes to friends, often on Sunday night, and served simple dishes, engendering a spirit of community and caring.

Although today's economy is much rosier than that of the thirties, entertaining is still a gesture of generosity, a ritual that connects us to each other. But it's hard to connect with your guests when you're fussing over dishes in the kitchen. With that in mind, we've designed 21 menus to get you out of the kitchen and into the living room. As the "Sunday night suppers" of the thirties showed us, meals centered around dishes such as Chicken Enchiladas and Honey-Mustard Pork Tenderloin are perfect for entertaining because spending time with company is more important than spending time in the kitchen.

**Green chiles add a spicy kick to Fiesta Burgers.**

Veal Steaks
With Caper Sauce

## Veal Steaks With Caper Sauce

2 tablespoons all-purpose flour
¼ teaspoon pepper
4 (4-ounce) boned veal loin steaks
   (1 inch thick)
Cooking spray
1 teaspoon olive oil
½ cup fat-free beef broth
1½ tablespoons capers
2 teaspoons Dijon mustard
½ cup fat-free sour cream
Chopped fresh parsley (optional)

**1.** Combine flour and pepper in a pie plate or shallow dish, and stir well. Dredge veal in flour mixture. Coat a large nonstick skillet with cooking spray; add oil, and place over medium-high heat until hot. Add veal, and cook 2 minutes on each side or until browned. Combine beef broth, capers, and mustard; stir until blended. Pour broth mixture over veal, and bring to a boil. Cover, reduce heat, and simmer 25 minutes or until veal is tender. Remove veal from skillet; set aside, and keep warm.

**2.** Bring broth mixture to a boil; cook, uncovered, over medium heat 5 minutes or until mixture is reduced by about half. Remove from heat; add sour cream, stirring with a whisk until blended. Spoon sauce evenly over veal. Garnish with parsley, if desired. Yield: 4 servings.

**POINTS**: 4; **Exchanges**: 3½ Very Lean Meat, ½ Starch, ½ Fat
**Per serving**: CAL 186 (27% from fat); PRO 25.7g; FAT 5.5g (sat 1.3g); CARB 5.4g; FIB 0.1g; CHOL 91mg; IRON 1.1mg; SOD 438mg; CALC 75mg

## Fiesta Burgers

Top grilled patties with this blend of highly seasoned ingredients and you have burgers "for adults only."

1⅓ cups seeded chopped tomato
¼ cup finely chopped onion
¼ cup taco sauce
1 (4.5-ounce) can chopped green chiles, drained
2 pounds ground round
2 tablespoons low-salt Worcestershire sauce
½ teaspoon ground cumin
¼ teaspoon onion powder
¼ teaspoon garlic powder

Cooking spray
8 curly leaf lettuce leaves
8 (1½-ounce) hamburger buns, split and toasted

**1.** Combine tomato, chopped onion, taco sauce, and green chiles in a small bowl; cover and chill 30 minutes.

**2.** Combine beef and next 4 ingredients in a large bowl; stir well. Divide mixture into 8 equal portions, shaping each into a 4-inch patty. Prepare grill or broiler. Place patties on a grill rack or broiler pan coated with cooking spray; cook 4 minutes on each side or until done.

**3.** Place lettuce leaves on bottom halves of buns; top with patties. Top evenly with tomato mixture and top halves of buns. Yield: 8 servings.

**POINTS**: 7; **Exchanges**: 3 Lean Meat, 1½ Starch, 1 Veg
**Per serving**: CAL 322 (26% from fat); PRO 28.6g; FAT 9.2g (sat 2.7g); CARB 29.1g; FIB 0.9g; CHOL 71.9mg; IRON 2.9mg; SOD 225mg; CALC 31.8mg

## Chicken Enchiladas

These easy saucy enchiladas received an enthusiastic thumbs-up from the Tex-Mex enthusiasts on our staff.

1¼ pounds skinned, boned chicken breasts
Cooking spray
1½ tablespoons chopped onion
1½ tablespoons chopped fresh cilantro
1 jalapeño pepper, seeded and minced
3 (10-ounce) cans enchilada sauce, divided
8 (6-inch) corn tortillas
1½ cups (6 ounces) shredded reduced-fat sharp cheddar cheese
½ cup diced tomato
⅓ cup sliced ripe olives
4 cups thinly sliced iceberg lettuce

**1.** Preheat oven to 350°.

**2.** Place chicken in a large saucepan, and cover with water; bring to a boil. Reduce heat to medium, and cook 15 minutes or until chicken is done. Drain; let cool slightly. Shred chicken with 2 forks; set aside.

**3.** Coat a large nonstick skillet with cooking spray, and place over medium-high heat until hot. Add onion, cilantro, and jalapeño, and sauté until onion is tender. Add shredded chicken and 1 can enchilada sauce, and cook 5 minutes, stirring occasionally.

**4.** Pour remaining 2 cans enchilada sauce into a small skillet; bring to a simmer. Dip corn tortillas, 1 at a time, into enchilada sauce; divide chicken mixture evenly among tortillas, and roll up. Place enchiladas, seam sides down, in a 13- x 9-inch baking dish. Pour warm enchilada sauce over enchiladas; sprinkle with cheese. Bake at 350° for 10 minutes or until enchiladas are thoroughly heated and cheese melts. Sprinkle evenly with tomato and olives. Serve each enchilada over ½ cup lettuce. Yield: 8 servings.

*POINTS:* 6; **Exchanges:** 2 Very Lean Meat, 1 Starch, 1 Veg, 1 Med-fat Meat, ½ Fat
**Per serving:** CAL 272 (32% from fat); PRO 24.7g; FAT 9.7g (sat 3.1g); CARB 21g; FIB 2.9g; CHOL 59mg; IRON 3.3mg; SOD 597mg; CALC 278mg

**Green chiles, lime, and cilantro add flavor to Mexican Butternut Squash Soup.**

## Herbed Pepper Steaks

2   (1-pound) lean flank steaks
2   tablespoons coarsely ground pepper
2   teaspoons dried Italian seasoning
1   teaspoon dry mustard
½   teaspoon garlic powder
Cooking spray

**1.** Trim fat from steaks. Combine pepper, Italian seasoning, mustard, and garlic powder; rub evenly over both sides of steaks.

**2.** Prepare grill. Place steaks on grill rack coated with cooking spray; grill 7 minutes on each side or until desired degree of doneness. Cut diagonally across grain into thin slices. Yield: 8 servings (serving size: 3 ounces).

*POINTS:* 4; **Exchanges:** 3½ Lean Meat
**Per serving:** CAL 183 (43% from fat); PRO 23.4g; FAT 8.8g (sat 3.7g); CARB 1.6g; FIB 0.5g; CHOL 57mg; IRON 3.1mg; SOD 72mg; CALC 24mg

## Mexican Butternut Squash Soup

This zesty soup is a good source of fiber.

2   teaspoons olive oil
2   cups peeled cubed butternut squash
    (about ¾ pound)
2   cups chopped onion
1   cup chopped red bell pepper
1   cup chopped celery
1   teaspoon dried oregano
1   teaspoon chili powder
1   (4.5-ounce) can chopped green chiles
4   cups canned vegetable broth
1   (15.5-ounce) can white hominy or
    whole-kernel corn, drained
¼   cup fresh lime juice
2   tablespoons minced fresh cilantro

**1.** Heat oil in a large Dutch oven over medium-high heat. Add squash and next 6 ingredients, and sauté 3 minutes. Add vegetable broth and hominy, and bring to a boil. Reduce heat, and simmer, uncovered, 35 minutes or until vegetables are tender. Remove from heat, and stir in lime juice and cilantro. Yield: 4 servings (serving size: 1¾ cups).

**Note:** You may substitute water for the canned vegetable broth. This will reduce the amount of sodium per serving by 1,000 milligrams.

*POINTS:* 3; **Exchanges:** 2 Starch, 1 Veg, ½ Fat
**Per serving:** CAL 203 (20% from fat); PRO 4.3g; FAT 4.4g (sat 0.4g); CARB 40.6g; FIB 5g; CHOL 0mg; IRON 1.9mg; SOD 1,244mg; CALC 84mg

## Chicken With Caramelized Onions

Although quick and easy to prepare, this dish is elegant enough for company.

Cooking spray
6   cups thinly sliced onion
½   teaspoon salt
¼   teaspoon dried thyme
¼   teaspoon ground red pepper
¼   teaspoon black pepper
½   cup low-salt chicken broth, divided
¼   cup balsamic vinegar
6   (4-ounce) skinned, boned chicken breast
    halves

**1.** Coat a large skillet with cooking spray; place over medium heat until hot. Add onion; cover and cook 10 minutes or until onion is golden brown, stirring frequently.

**2.** Combine salt and next 3 ingredients; stir well. Sprinkle half of spice mixture over onions; add ¼ cup chicken broth, and cook 10 minutes, stirring frequently. Add 2 tablespoons broth, and cook until liquid evaporates, scraping pan to loosen browned bits. Stir in remaining 2 tablespoons broth; cook until liquid evaporates. Add vinegar, and cook an additional 2 minutes or until liquid almost evaporates. Remove onion mixture from skillet; set aside, and keep warm. Wipe skillet clean with paper towels.

**3.** Rub chicken with remaining spice mixture. Recoat skillet with cooking spray; place over medium-high heat until hot. Add chicken; cook 5 minutes on each side or until done. Serve chicken with caramelized onion mixture. Yield: 6 servings (serving size: 1 chicken breast half and ⅓ cup onion mixture).

*POINTS:* 4; **Exchanges:** 3½ Very Lean Meat, 1 Veg, ½ Starch
**Per serving:** CAL 193 (19% from fat); PRO 27.7g; FAT 4g (sat 1.1g); CARB 10.3g; FIB 2.2g; CHOL 72mg; IRON 1.3mg; SOD 305mg; CALC 38mg

## Sesame-Baked Orange Roughy

Baking or broiling is the best cooking method for delicate fish, such as orange roughy.

2½  tablespoons water
1½  teaspoons peeled minced fresh ginger
¾   teaspoon lemon juice
¾   teaspoon low-salt soy sauce
¼   teaspoon crushed red pepper
1   garlic clove, minced
6   (6-ounce) orange roughy fillets
3   tablespoons sesame seeds, toasted
Cooking spray
¼   teaspoon paprika
Lemon slices (optional)

**1.** Place first 6 ingredients in a blender; process until smooth. Pour mixture into a shallow baking dish; add fish, turning to coat. Cover; marinate in refrigerator 1 to 2 hours, turning occasionally.

**2.** Remove fish fillets from dish, and discard marinade. Place sesame seeds in a pie plate or shallow dish, and dredge fish in sesame seeds.

**3.** Place fish on a broiler pan coated with cooking spray, and broil 6 minutes or until fish flakes easily when tested with a fork. Sprinkle evenly with paprika; garnish with lemon slices, if desired. Yield: 6 servings.

*POINTS:* 3; **Exchanges:** 3½ Very Lean Meat, ½ Fat
**Per serving:** CAL 142 (22% from fat); PRO 25g; FAT 3.4g (sat 0.3g); CARB 1.5g; FIB 0.3g; CHOL 33mg; IRON 1.0mg; SOD 12.6mg; CALC 45mg

## Yogurt-Marinated Lamb Kabobs

1½  pounds lean, boned leg of lamb
¾   cup plain fat-free yogurt
1½  tablespoons ground cumin
3    tablespoons finely chopped onion
2    tablespoons olive oil
1½  teaspoons dried rosemary
1½  teaspoons pepper
¾   teaspoon salt
3    garlic cloves, minced
6    cups (1-inch-thick) sliced zucchini
18   large cherry tomatoes
3    small onions, quartered
Cooking spray
6    cups hot cooked couscous, cooked without
     salt or fat

**1.** Trim fat from lamb. Cut lamb into 1-inch pieces; set aside.

**2.** Combine yogurt and next 7 ingredients in a large zip-top plastic bag. Add lamb, zucchini, tomatoes, and onion wedges; seal and refrigerate 8 hours, turning bag occasionally. Remove lamb and vegetables from bag, reserving marinade.

**3.** Thread lamb onto each of 6 (10-inch) skewers. Thread vegetables alternately onto each of 6 (10-inch) skewers. Prepare grill or broiler. Place kabobs on grill rack or broiler pan coated with cooking spray. Cook 14 minutes or until lamb is done, turning and basting occasionally with reserved marinade. Serve kabobs over couscous. Yield: 6 servings (serving size: 1 lamb kabob, 1 vegetable kabob, and 1 cup couscous).

*POINTS:* 9; **Exchanges:** 3 Starch, 3½ Lean Meat, 1 Veg, ½ Fat
**Per serving:** CAL 464 (25% from fat); PRO 35.4g; FAT 12.8g (sat 3.1g); CARB 53.1g; FIB 4.3g; CHOL 76mg; IRON 5mg; SOD 390mg; CALC 116mg

## Sacramento Taco Soup

1    pound skinned, boned chicken breasts, cut
     into bite-size pieces
2    (14.5-ounce) cans no-salt-added whole
     tomatoes, undrained and chopped
2    (14¼-ounce) cans fat-free chicken broth
1    (4.5-ounce) can chopped green chiles,
     undrained
¼   teaspoon salt
4    (6-inch) corn tortillas, halved

½ cup chopped green onions

½ cup (2 ounces) shredded reduced-fat
  Monterey Jack cheese

¼ cup chopped fresh cilantro

¼ cup green taco sauce

**1.** Combine first 5 ingredients in a large sauce-pan; bring to a boil. Reduce heat, and simmer, uncovered, 30 minutes.

**2.** Tear each tortilla half into 1-inch pieces; place 1 torn tortilla half into each of 8 soup bowls. Ladle soup into bowls; top each with 1 table-spoon green onions, 1 tablespoon cheese, 1½ tea-spoons cilantro, and 1½ teaspoons green taco sauce. Yield: 8 servings (serving size: 1 cup).

*POINTS:* 3; **Exchanges:** 2 Very Lean Meat, 1 Starch
**Per serving:** CAL 155 (17% from fat); PRO 17.4g; FAT 2.9g (sat 1.1g); CARB 13.2g; FIB 1.7g; CHOL 38mg; IRON 1.8mg; SOD 277mg; CALC 130mg

**Sacramento Taco Soup is loaded with savory toppings.**

Greek-Seasoned
Chicken With Orzo

## Greek-Seasoned Chicken With Orzo

¼  cup fresh lemon juice
3  tablespoons water
1  teaspoon olive oil
½  teaspoon dried oregano
½  teaspoon Greek-style seasoning
¼  teaspoon pepper
2  garlic cloves, crushed
4  (6-ounce) skinned chicken breast halves
Cooking spray
3  cups hot cooked orzo (about 1 cup uncooked rice-shaped pasta), cooked without salt or fat
¼  cup sliced ripe olives
1½ tablespoons chopped fresh chives
1  tablespoon reduced-calorie stick margarine, melted
¾  teaspoon Greek-style seasoning
Oregano sprigs (optional)

1. Combine first 7 ingredients in a large heavy-duty zip-top plastic bag. Add chicken; seal and marinate in refrigerator 30 minutes.

2. Remove chicken from bag, reserving marinade. Prepare grill. Place chicken on grill rack coated with cooking spray; cover and grill 10 minutes on each side or until chicken is done, basting occasionally with reserved marinade.

3. Combine orzo and next 4 ingredients in a bowl; toss gently to coat. Divide orzo mixture evenly among individual plates; place chicken breasts on top of orzo. Garnish with oregano sprigs, if desired. Yield: 4 servings.

POINTS: 9; Exchanges: 5 Very Lean Meat, 2½ Starch, 1 Fat
Per serving: CAL 420 (19% from fat); PRO 43.9g; FAT 9g (sat 1.9g); CARB 38.6g; FIB 1.6g; CHOL 102mg; IRON 3.8mg; SOD 476mg; CALC 38mg

## Minted-Molasses Pork Tenderloin

Serve with wild rice for a simple but elegant meal.

2  (1-pound) pork tenderloins
⅓  cup molasses
¼  cup minced fresh mint
1  tablespoon peeled grated fresh ginger
3  tablespoons low-salt soy sauce
3  tablespoons hoisin sauce
2  tablespoons water
2  garlic cloves, minced
Cooking spray

1. Trim fat from pork; set aside.

2. Combine molasses and next 6 ingredients in a large zip-top plastic bag. Add pork to bag; seal and marinate in refrigerator 8 hours, turning bag occasionally. Remove pork from bag, reserving marinade. Insert meat thermometer into thickest portion of 1 tenderloin.

3. Prepare grill. Place pork on grill rack coated with cooking spray; grill 20 minutes or until thermometer registers 160° (slightly pink), turning and basting occasionally with reserved marinade. Yield: 8 servings (serving size: 3 ounces).

POINTS: 4; Exchanges: 3 Very Lean Meat, 1 Starch
Per serving: CAL 186 (20% from fat); PRO 25.3g; FAT 4.2g (sat 1.4g); CARB 10.5g; FIB 0.1g; CHOL 79mg; IRON 2.3mg; SOD 319mg; CALC 36mg

## Pasta-and-Bean Soup

Make sure you use the hot pepper sauce that has green chile peppers packed in vinegar, not the red hot sauce.

Cooking spray
1  tablespoon olive oil
1  cup chopped onion
1  cup sliced carrot
½  cup chopped green bell pepper
2  garlic cloves, minced
2  (14½-ounce) cans vegetable broth
1  (28-ounce) can crushed tomatoes, undrained
1  (15-ounce) can chickpeas (garbanzo beans), drained
1  (16-ounce) can red beans, rinsed and drained
1½ teaspoons dried Italian seasoning
½  teaspoon salt
½  teaspoon hot pepper sauce
¼  teaspoon pepper
6  ounces uncooked elbow macaroni
½  cup (2 ounces) grated fresh Parmesan cheese

1. Coat a large Dutch oven with cooking spray; add oil, and place over medium-high heat until hot. Add chopped onion and next 3 ingredients; sauté until vegetables are crisp-tender. Add vegetable broth and next 7 ingredients; bring mixture to a boil. Cover, reduce heat to low, and simmer 20 minutes, stirring occasionally. Add

*O*rzo is a tiny rice-shaped pasta that expands to three times its volume when cooked. Ideal for soups, orzo also may be served as a substitute for rice.

**1** Cook 1 cup of orzo in 3 quarts of boiling water, without salt or fat, for 8 minutes. Rinse cooked orzo in hot water to keep the pieces from sticking together once cooked.

**2** Toss together orzo, olives, chives, margarine, and Greek-style seasoning. Serve as a side dish to grilled or broiled chicken, lamb, or tuna. To turn this into a main dish, stir in chopped cooked lamb or chicken and crumbled feta cheese.

**Topped with golden breadcrumbs, Flounder With Dill is an easy but elegant entrée for company.**

pasta; cover and cook 10 minutes or until pasta is done. Ladle soup into bowls; top each serving with 1 tablespoon cheese. Yield 8 servings (serving size: 1¼ cup).

*POINTS:* 4; **Exchanges:** 2 Starch, 1 Veg, ½ Lean Meat, ½ Fat
**Per serving:** CAL 232 (17% from fat); PRO 10.8g; FAT 4.5g (sat 1.5g); CARB 36.2g; FIB 4.2g; CHOL 5mg; IRON 3.3mg; SOD 497mg; CALC 152mg

## Ginger-Lime Mahimahi

½   cup fresh lime juice
2   tablespoons honey
2   garlic cloves, minced
2   (⅛-inch-thick) slices peeled fresh ginger
8   (6-ounce) mahimahi or other firm white fish fillets (about ¾ inch thick)
Cooking spray

**1.** Combine lime juice, honey, garlic, and ginger in a large shallow dish; add fish fillets, turning to coat. Cover and marinate in refrigerator 1 hour, turning fish occasionally.

**2.** Remove fish from dish, reserving marinade. Remove and discard ginger. Prepare grill. Place fish on grill rack coated with cooking spray; grill 8 minutes on each side or until fish flakes easily when tested with a fork, basting frequently with reserved marinade. Yield: 8 servings.

*POINTS:* 3; **Exchanges:** 4 Very Lean Meat, ½ Starch
**Per serving:** CAL 163 (7% from fat); PRO 30.5g; FAT 1.3g (sat 0g); CARB 6.1g; FIB 0g; CHOL 73mg; IRON 0.7mg; SOD 104mg; CALC 22mg

## Flounder With Dill

4   small tomatoes, cut into ¼-inch-thick slices
Cooking spray
4   (6-ounce) flounder fillets
6   tablespoons dry breadcrumbs
1½ tablespoons grated Parmesan cheese
2¼ teaspoons chopped fresh dill
¼   teaspoon salt
⅛   teaspoon white pepper
⅛   teaspoon ground red pepper
1½ tablespoons stick margarine, melted
Dill sprigs (optional)

**1.** Preheat oven to 425°.

**2.** Place tomato slices in a 13- x 9-inch baking dish coated with cooking spray; arrange fish on top of tomatoes. Combine breadcrumbs and next 5 ingredients in a small bowl; stir in margarine. Sprinkle breadcrumb mixture evenly over fish.

**3.** Bake at 425° for 13 minutes or until fish flakes easily when tested with a fork. Garnish with dill sprigs, if desired. Yield: 4 servings (serving size: 1 fish fillet and 1 tomato).

*POINTS:* 5; **Exchanges:** 4½ Very Lean Meat, 1½ Fat, ½ Starch
**Per serving:** CAL 256 (27% from fat); PRO 33.7g; FAT 7.6g (sat 1.8g); CARB 11.8g; FIB 1.6g; CHOL 88mg; IRON 1.5mg; SOD 461mg; CALC 79mg

## Hoisin Pork Medallions

Cooking spray
1   tablespoon dark sesame oil
¼ to ½ teaspoon crushed red pepper
3   garlic cloves, minced
1   (1-pound) pork tenderloin, cut crosswise into ½-inch-thick slices
6   tablespoons water
⅓   cup dry sherry
3   tablespoons chopped fresh cilantro
3   tablespoons hoisin sauce
2   cups hot cooked long-grain rice, cooked without salt or fat
¼   cup sliced green onions
Cilantro sprigs (optional)

**1.** Coat a nonstick skillet with cooking spray; add oil, and place over medium-high heat until hot. Add pepper and garlic; sauté 1 minute. Add pork; cook 4 minutes on each side or until browned. Remove pork from skillet. Wipe drippings from skillet with a paper towel.

**2.** Combine water and next 3 ingredients in skillet; cook over medium heat 1 minute, stirring constantly. Return pork to skillet, turning to coat. Place rice on a platter; spoon pork mixture over rice, and sprinkle with green onions. Garnish with cilantro sprigs, if desired. Yield: 4 servings (serving size: 3 ounces pork and ½ cup rice).

**POINTS:** 7; **Exchanges:** 3 Very Lean Meat, 2 Starch, 1 Fat
**Per serving:** CAL 303 (23% from fat); PRO 27.1g; FAT 7.9g (sat 1.9g); CARB 29.1g; FIB 1g; CHOL 79mg; IRON 2.6mg; SOD 195mg; CALC 34mg

## Cornish Hens With Rosemary-Wine Sauce

Using an electric knife makes it easier to cut Cornish hens or chickens in half.

2    (1-pound) Cornish hens
Cooking spray
1    cup dry white wine
⅓    cup white wine vinegar
2    tablespoons low-salt soy sauce
1    teaspoon dried rosemary
¼    teaspoon dried thyme
4    garlic cloves, minced

**1.** Preheat oven to 350°.

**2.** Remove and discard giblets and necks from hens. Rinse hens under cold water; pat dry. Remove skin; trim excess fat. Split each hen in half lengthwise. Place hens, meaty sides up, in a 13- x 9-inch baking dish coated with cooking spray.

**3.** Combine wine and next 5 ingredients; pour over hens. Bake, uncovered, at 350° for 1 hour or until juices run clear, basting occasionally with wine mixture. Yield: 4 servings.

**POINTS:** 4; **Exchanges:** 2 Lean Meat, 2 Very Lean Meat
**Per serving:** CAL 185 (33% from fat); PRO 26.2g; FAT 6.8g (sat 1.8g); CARB 2g; FIB 0.1g; CHOL 80mg; IRON 1.6mg; SOD 279mg; CALC 29mg

**Hoisin Pork Medallions are coated in a spicy-sweet brown sauce.**

Veal Cordon Bleu

## Veal Cordon Bleu

8  (2-ounce) lean veal cutlets
½  teaspoon freshly ground pepper
2  (¾-ounce) slices fat-free Swiss processed cheese, each slice cut in half
1  (1-ounce) slice lean ham, cut into 4 equal pieces
2  tablespoons all-purpose flour
6  tablespoons egg substitute
½  cup dry breadcrumbs
Cooking spray
1  tablespoon reduced-calorie stick margarine
Parsley sprigs (optional)
Lemon slices (optional)

**1.** Preheat oven to 375°.

**2.** Place each veal cutlet between 2 sheets of heavy-duty plastic wrap. Flatten to ⅛-inch thickness using a meat mallet or rolling pin. Sprinkle freshly ground pepper evenly over 4 cutlets.

**3.** Place 1 half-slice Swiss cheese in center of each of 4 peppered cutlets; top each cutlet with a piece of lean ham. Place remaining 4 cutlets over ham, pressing edges gently to seal.

**4.** Dredge cutlets in flour, and shake off excess flour. Dip each cutlet in egg substitute, then dredge in breadcrumbs.

**5.** Coat a large nonstick skillet with cooking spray; add stick margarine, and place over medium-high heat until margarine melts. Add cutlets and cook 2 minutes on each side or until cutlet are lightly browned. Place cutlets in an 11- x 7-inch baking dish coated with cooking spray. Bake, uncovered, at 375° for 20 minutes. Garnish with parsley sprigs and lemon slices, if desired. Yield: 4 servings.

*POINTS:* 6; **Exchanges:** 3½ Very Lean Meat, 1 Starch
**Per serving:** CAL 267 (30% from fat); PRO 30.4g; FAT 8.8g (sat 2.9g); CARB 15.2g; FIB 0.7g; CHOL 95mg; IRON 2.1mg; SOD 582mg; CALC 134mg

## Chicken in Port

Cooking spray
2¾  cups quartered fresh mushrooms
1  teaspoon stick margarine
1  pound skinned, boned chicken breasts, cut into 1-inch pieces
¼  cup tawny port or other sweet red wine
¼  cup no-sugar-added black cherry spread
¼  teaspoon salt
¼  teaspoon pepper
⅛  teaspoon dried thyme
2  cups hot cooked long-grain rice, cooked without salt or fat

**1.** Coat a large nonstick skillet with cooking spray; place over medium-high heat until hot. Add fresh mushrooms, and sauté 10 minutes. Remove mushrooms from skillet, and set aside.

**2.** Melt margarine in skillet over medium-high heat. Add chicken breast, and sauté 12 minutes or until chicken is no longer pink. Add wine, and cook 3 minutes, stirring constantly. Return mushrooms to skillet; stir in black cherry spread, salt, pepper, and dried thyme. Reduce heat, and simmer, uncovered, until thoroughly heated. Serve over rice. Yield: 4 servings (serving size: ¾ cup chicken and ½ cup rice).

*POINTS:* 6; **Exchanges:** 3½ Very Lean Meat, 2 Starch
**Per serving:** CAL 279 (9% from fat); PRO 29.3g; FAT 2.9g (sat 0.8g); CARB 32.1g; FIB 1.1g; CHOL 66mg; IRON 2.4mg; SOD 236mg; CALC 26mg

## Honey-Mustard Pork Tenderloin

2  (½-pound) pork tenderloins
¼  teaspoon salt
⅛  teaspoon pepper
Cooking spray
1  teaspoon olive oil
¼  cup balsamic vinegar
1  tablespoon honey
1  teaspoon Dijon mustard
1  teaspoon chopped fresh rosemary
Lemon wedges (optional)
Rosemary sprigs (optional)

**1.** Preheat oven to 400°.

**2.** Trim fat from pork tenderloins; rub pork with salt and pepper. Coat a large nonstick skillet with cooking spray; add oil, and place over medium-high heat until hot. Add pork, and cook 10 minutes, turning and browning on all sides.

**3.** Place pork on a broiler pan coated with cooking spray. Combine balsamic vinegar, honey, and Dijon mustard in a small bowl, and stir well

¼ teaspoon pepper
4 (4-ounce) skinned, boned chicken breast halves
1 tablespoon cornstarch
2 teaspoons water
Tarragon sprigs (optional)

**1.** Combine mushrooms, wine, parsley, tarragon, salt, and pepper in a large nonstick skillet, and bring to a boil over high heat. Add chicken breast; cover, reduce heat, and simmer 20 minutes or until chicken is done. Remove chicken from skillet with a slotted spoon; set aside, and keep warm.

**2.** Combine cornstarch and water in a small bowl, and stir well. Add cornstarch mixture to wine mixture; bring to a boil, and cook 1 minute, stirring constantly. Pour sauce evenly over chicken. Garnish with tarragon sprigs, if desired. Yield: 4 servings.

*POINTS:* 3; **Exchanges:** 4 Very Lean Meat
**Per serving:** CAL 147 (10% from fat); PRO 27.4g; FAT 1.6g (sat 0.4g); CARB 4.7g; FIB 0.8g; CHOL 66mg; IRON 1.7mg; SOD 372mg; CALC 11mg

---

**Serve Wine-Poached Chicken with fettuccine and asparagus.**

with whisk. Brush vinegar mixture over pork. Insert a meat thermometer into thickest portion of 1 tenderloin.

**4.** Bake tenderloin at 400° for 30 minutes or until thermometer registers 160° (slightly pink), basting frequently with vinegar mixture. Place tenderloins on a serving platter, and sprinkle with chopped fresh rosemary. Garnish with lemon wedges and rosemary sprigs, if desired. Yield: 4 servings (serving size: 3 ounces).

*POINTS:* 4; **Exchanges:** 3½ Very Lean Meat, ½ Starch
**Per serving:** CAL 174 (29% from fat); PRO 24.5g; FAT 5.6g (sat 1.6g); CARB 5.3g; FIB 0g; CHOL 79mg; IRON 1.4mg; SOD 241mg; CALC 10mg

## Wine-Poached Chicken

2½ cups sliced fresh mushrooms
¾ cup dry white wine
2 tablespoons chopped fresh parsley
1½ teaspoons chopped fresh or ½ teaspoon dried tarragon
½ teaspoon salt

## Lemon-Garlic Beef Steaks

2 tablespoons minced fresh parsley
1½ teaspoons grated lemon rind
¾ teaspoon cracked black pepper
3 garlic cloves, minced
6 (4-ounce) filet mignon steaks (about 1 inch thick)
Cooking spray
½ teaspoon salt

**1.** Combine parsley, lemon rind, pepper, and garlic in a small bowl, and stir well. Rub mixture evenly over both sides of filet mignon steaks. Coat a large nonstick skillet with cooking spray, and place over medium-high heat until hot. Sprinkle skillet with salt; add steaks, and cook 5 minutes on each side or until desired degree of doneness. Yield: 6 servings (serving size: 3 ounces).

*POINTS:* 4; **Exchanges:** 3½ Lean Meat
**Per serving:** CAL 179 (41% from fat); PRO 24.2g; FAT 8.1g (sat 3g); CARB 0.8g; FIB 0.1g; CHOL 71mg; IRON 3.2mg; SOD 250mg; CALC 12mg

*Serves 6*

Yogurt-Marinated Lamb Kabobs, page 52

Chickpea Dip, page 19

Minted Cucumber-Sprout Nests, page 75

Pineapple-Cheese Pudding, page 87

*Serves 4*

Greek-Seasoned Chicken With Orzo, page 55

Chickpea Dip, page 19

Artichoke-Feta Green Salad, page 73

Pink Grapefruit-and-Tarragon Sorbet, page 84

*Serves 4*

Veal Steaks With Caper Sauce, page 49

rice pilaf (generic)

Artichoke-Feta Green Salad, page 73

Almond-Dusted Strawberries, page 82

*Serves 6*

Sesame-Baked Orange Roughy, page 51

tossed green salad (generic)

Vegetable-Rice Toss, page 66

Orange Drop Biscuits, page 66

Strawberry-Yogurt Layer Cake, page 88

*Serves 8*

Ginger-Lime Mahimahi, page 56

Simple Sesame Spinach, page 75

Vegetable-Rice Toss, page 66

Cherry-Yogurt Parfaits, page 81

*Serves 4*

Wine-Poached Chicken, page 60

cooked fettuccine (generic)

steamed asparagus (generic)

Pink Grapefruit-and-Tarragon Sorbet,
page 84

*Serves 4*

Veal Cordon Bleu, page 59

steamed green beans (generic)

baked potatoes (generic)

Pink Grapefruit-and-Tarragon Sorbet,
page 84

*Serves 8*

Minted-Molasses Pork Tenderloin, page 55

Oriental Crab Spread, page 71

steamed broccoli (generic)

cooked wild rice (generic)

Chewy Lemon Wafers, page 81

*Serves 4*

Honey-Mustard Pork Tenderloin, page 59

steamed baby carrots (generic)

Lemon Couscous, page 12

Apple-Berry Crisp, page 83

*Serves 4*

Mexican Butternut Squash Soup, page 51

Creamy Guacamole and Chips, page 75

reduced-fat cheese quesadillas (generic)

Frozen Chocolate Brownie Pie, page 87

*Serves 4*

Hoisin Pork Medallions, page 56

steamed carrot sticks (generic)

whole-wheat dinner rolls (generic)

Ginger-Berry Shortcakes, page 84

*Serves 4*

Flounder With Dill, page 56

Lemon Couscous, page 12

tossed green salad (generic)

Pound Cake, page 89, served with fresh
fruit

*Serves 6*

Lemon-Garlic Beef Steaks, page 60

steamed asparagus (generic)

baked potatoes (generic)

Creamy Amaretto Dip, page 84, served
with fresh fruit

*Serves 8*

Chicken Enchiladas, page 49

Southwestern Rice, page 68

Jicama-Orange Salad, page 76

Kahlúa-Cinnamon Brownies, page 88

*Serves 8*

Fiesta Burgers, page 49

Tex-Mex Black Bean Dip, page 65

Ranch Slaw, page 71

Raspberry-Chocolate Soda, page 88

*Serves 6*

Chicken With Caramelized Onions, page 51

wild rice pilaf (generic)

steamed asparagus (generic)

Lemon-Poppy Seed Cake, page 84

*Serves 4*

Cornish Hens With Rosemary-Wine
Sauce, page 57

Honey Mustard-Whipped Sweet Potatoes,
page 72

steamed green beans (generic)

Cappuccino Pudding Cake, page 81

*Serves 8*

Pasta-and-Bean Soup, page 55

Cauliflower Medley, page 71

Cheddar-Black Pepper Biscuits, page 73

Peaches Amaretto, page 90

*Serves 4*

Chicken in Port, page 59

steamed green beans (generic)

dinner rolls (generic)

Frozen Chocolate Brownie Pie, page 87

*Serves 8*

Herbed Pepper Steaks, page 50

Mushroom Pilaf, page 72

Garlic-Basil Squash, page 72

Peaches Amaretto, page 90

*Serves 8*

Sacramento Taco Soup, page 52

Tex-Mex Black Bean Dip, page 65

Spicy Lettuce Salad, page 71

Easy Chocolate-Caramel Brownies,
page 19

# Balance of Power

As good as it is, roasted chicken is not a meal unto itself. Neither is steamed broccoli, or rice, or French bread for that matter. A meal should be well balanced—and although it's an idea we don't give much thought to, in the back of our minds we know that ideally dinner consists of a protein-rich entrée, a starch, and a green vegetable. But who has time to follow three or more recipes for an everyday meal? No one we know. That's why we suggest this strategy: Rather than cut nutritional corners, pick one recipe to anchor the meal and make the other dishes generic. And every once in a while, let the side dish steal the show. For instance, prepare Garlic-Basil Squash and serve it with a grilled chicken breast and rice, or try Chili-Corn Mashed Potatoes with flank steak and sliced tomatoes. After all, the entrée doesn't always have to be the center of attention.

**Use a bag of precut florets to make Easy Citrus Broccoli even faster.**

Tex-Mex Black Bean Dip

## Easy Citrus Broccoli

Steamed fresh broccoli tastes great on its own, but a simple sauce can magnify its appeal.

4   cups fresh broccoli florets
1   tablespoon reduced-calorie stick margarine
1   tablespoon all-purpose flour
1   teaspoon grated orange rind
¾   cup fresh orange juice

**1.** Steam broccoli, covered, 3 minutes or until crisp-tender. Spoon into a serving bowl; set aside, and keep warm.

**2.** Melt margarine over medium heat in a small saucepan. Stir in flour; cook 1 minute, stirring constantly. Gradually add orange rind and juice; cook until thick and bubbly, stirring constantly. Spoon sauce over broccoli. Yield: 4 servings (serving size: 1 cup).

*POINTS:* 1; *Exchanges:* 2 Veg, ½ Fat
**Per serving:** CAL 68 (29% from fat); PRO 3.1g; FAT 2.2g (sat 0.3g); CARB 11.2g; FIB 2.9g; CHOL 0mg; IRON 0.9mg; SOD 52mg; CALC 48mg

## Fruity Banana Bread

We took a yummy banana bread recipe, stirred in some chopped dried fruit, and came up with this quick bread that goes great with chicken salad.

⅓   cup stick margarine, softened
¾   cup sugar
½   cup egg substitute
1¾   cups all-purpose flour
2¾   teaspoons baking powder
1   cup mashed ripe banana (about 2 medium)
¾   cup coarsely chopped dried mixed fruit
Cooking spray

**1.** Preheat oven to 350°.

**2.** Cream margarine; gradually add sugar, beating at medium speed of a mixer until well blended. Add egg substitute, beating just until blended.

**3.** Combine flour and baking powder in a bowl; stir well. Add flour mixture to margarine mixture; beat at low speed just until blended. Stir in banana and dried fruit.

**4.** Spoon batter into an 8½- x 4½-inch loaf pan coated with cooking spray. Bake at 350° for 1 hour or until a wooden pick inserted in center comes out clean. Let cool in pan on a wire rack 10 minutes and remove from pan. Let cool completely on wire rack. Yield: 16 servings (serving size: 1 slice).

*POINTS:* 3; *Exchanges:* 1 Starch, 1 Fruit, ½ Fat
**Per serving:** CAL 150 (24% from fat); PRO 2.2g; FAT 4g (sat 0.8g); CARB 27.3g; FIB 1.5g; CHOL 0mg; IRON 1.1mg; SOD 64mg; CALC 56mg

## Tex-Mex Black Bean Dip

This recipe received the highest rating given in our *WWM* test kitchens.

1   (15-ounce) can black beans, drained
1   teaspoon vegetable oil
½   cup chopped onion
2   garlic cloves, minced
½   cup diced tomato
⅓   cup picante sauce
½   teaspoon ground cumin
½   teaspoon chili powder
¼   cup (1 ounce) shredded reduced-fat Monterey Jack cheese
¼   cup chopped fresh cilantro
1   tablespoon fresh lime juice

**1.** Place beans in a bowl; partially mash with a fork. Set aside.

**2.** Heat oil in a nonstick skillet over medium heat. Add onion and garlic; sauté 4 minutes. Add beans, tomato, picante sauce, cumin, and chili powder; cook 5 minutes or until thick, stirring constantly. Remove from heat; stir in cheese, cilantro, and lime juice. Serve warm or at room temperature with baked tortilla chips. Yield: 13 servings (serving size: 2 tablespoons).

*POINTS:* 1; *Exchanges:* ½ Starch
**Per serving:** CAL 42 (21% from fat); PRO 2.6g; FAT 1g (sat 0.4g); CARB 6.2g; FIB 1g; CHOL 2mg; IRON 0.6mg; SOD 136mg; CALC 30mg

## Cheesy Garlic Bread

1   (1-pound) loaf unsliced Italian bread
Butter-flavored cooking spray
¼   cup grated Parmesan cheese
1   tablespoon minced fresh parsley
¼   teaspoon garlic powder

**1.** Preheat oven to 350°.

**2.** Slice bread loaf in half horizontally; coat cut sides of bread with cooking spray. Combine

## LOW-FAT DROP BISCUITS

*T*raditionally, vegetable shortening or lard has been used as the fat in biscuits. However, these products are almost never used in low-fat recipes because of their extremely high saturated fat content. Vegetable oil may sometimes be used in place of shortening, and reduced-calorie and regular margarines are often substituted.

**Preparing drop biscuits is easy—just combine the ingredients, and then drop the dough by spoonfuls onto a baking sheet.**

cheese, parsley, and garlic powder; sprinkle over bottom half of bread, and replace top half of bread.

**3.** Wrap loaf in foil; bake at 350° for 20 minutes or until bread is thoroughly heated. Cut loaf crosswise into 20 (½-inch) slices. Yield: 20 servings (serving size: 1 slice).

**POINTS:** 1; **Exchanges:** 1 Starch
**Per serving:** CAL 69 (8% from fat); PRO 2.6g; FAT 0.6g (sat 0.4g); CARB 12.9g; FIB 0.6g; CHOL 1mg; IRON 0.5mg; SOD 156mg; CALC 21mg

### Orange Drop Biscuits

1¼ cups all-purpose flour
1 tablespoon sugar
1½ teaspoons baking powder
¼ teaspoon baking soda
3 tablespoons chilled reduced-calorie stick margarine, cut into small pieces
⅓ cup 1% low-fat cottage cheese
¼ cup egg substitute
3 tablespoons low-sugar orange marmalade
¾ teaspoon grated orange rind
Cooking spray

**1.** Preheat oven to 400°.

**2.** Combine first 4 ingredients in a bowl; cut in margarine with a pastry blender or 2 knives until mixture resembles coarse meal. Combine cottage cheese and next 3 ingredients in a bowl; stir well. Add cheese mixture to dry ingredients, stirring just until moist.

**3.** Drop dough by rounded tablespoonfuls onto a baking sheet coated with cooking spray. Bake at 400° for 8 minutes or until golden. Yield: 2 dozen (serving size: 1 biscuit).

**POINTS:** 1; **Exchanges:** ½ Starch
**Per serving:** CAL 38 (24% from fat); PRO 1.3g; FAT 1.0g (sat 0.9g); CARB 5.8g; FIB 0.2g; CHOL 0mg; IRON 0.4mg; SOD 74mg; CALC 22mg

### Rancher's Beans

Cooking spray
¼ cup chopped green bell pepper
1 (16-ounce) can vegetarian baked beans
1 (15-ounce) can kidney beans, drained
¼ cup no-salt-added tomato sauce
2 tablespoons molasses

1 tablespoon yellow mustard
¼ teaspoon onion powder

**1.** Coat a medium saucepan with cooking spray; place over medium-high heat until hot. Add bell pepper; sauté 3 minutes. Add baked beans and remaining ingredients. Reduce heat, and simmer, uncovered, 10 minutes or until thoroughly heated. Yield: 6 servings (serving size: ½ cup).

**POINTS:** 2; **Exchanges:** 2 Starch
**Per serving:** CAL 125 (2% from fat); PRO 6g; FAT 0.7g (sat 0g); CARB 25.5g; FIB 8.1g; CHOL 0mg; IRON 2.2mg; SOD 494mg; CALC 67mg

### Vegetable-Rice Toss

Five-spice powder is a pungent mixture of ground cinnamon, cloves, fennel seed, star anise, and Szechuan peppercorns. Look for it on the ethnic aisle of your supermarket near the Asian products or displayed with the other spices.

Cooking spray
1 teaspoon dark sesame oil
¾ cup chopped onion
½ cup diced carrot
2 garlic cloves, minced
2 (10½-ounce) cans low-salt chicken broth
¼ teaspoon salt
¼ teaspoon five-spice powder
¼ teaspoon pepper
1¼ cups uncooked long-grain rice
½ cup frozen green peas, thawed
½ cup sliced green onions
Sliced green onion tops (optional)

**1.** Coat a large nonstick skillet with cooking spray; add dark sesame oil, and place over medium-high heat until hot. Add chopped onion, carrot, and minced garlic cloves; sauté 5 minutes or until tender. Stir in broth, salt, five-spice powder, and pepper, and bring to a boil. Add rice; return to a boil. Cover, reduce heat, and simmer 20 minutes or until liquid is absorbed. Remove from heat. Add peas and ½ cup green onions; toss gently. Garnish with sliced green onion tops, if desired. Yield 8 servings (serving size: ⅔ cup).

**POINTS:** 3; **Exchanges:** 1½ Starch, 1 Veg
**Per serving:** CAL 139 (8% from fat); PRO 3.6g; FAT 1.3g (sat 0.2g); CARB 27.7g; FIB 1.3g; CHOL 0mg; IRON 1.6mg; SOD 113mg; CALC 22mg

## Tropical Carrot-Raisin Salad

¼  cup vanilla low-fat yogurt
2  tablespoons fat-free mayonnaise
1½  teaspoons creamy peanut butter
⅛  teaspoon ground cinnamon
2  cups shredded carrot
6  tablespoons raisins
1  (8-ounce) can crushed pineapple in juice,
   drained

**1.** Combine yogurt, mayonnaise, peanut butter, and cinnamon in a medium bowl, and stir well. Add carrot, raisins, and pineapple, and toss gently to coat. Cover and chill. Yield: 6 servings (serving size: ½ cup).

*POINTS:* 1; **Exchanges:** 1 Fruit, 1 Veg
**Per serving:** CAL 85 (10% from fat); PRO 1.7g; FAT 0.9g (sat 0.2g); CARB 19.1g; FIB 2.1g; CHOL 0mg; IRON 0.5mg; SOD 91mg; CALC 36mg

## Mint-Glazed Potatoes

12  small red potatoes (about 1½ pounds)
1  tablespoon stick margarine
1  tablespoon sugar
1  tablespoon minced fresh mint
1  teaspoon balsamic vinegar

**1.** Steam potatoes, covered, 20 minutes or until tender; drain. Place potatoes in bowl; set aside, and keep warm.

**2.** Melt margarine over medium heat. Add sugar; cook 1 minute, stirring constantly. Remove from heat; stir in mint and vinegar. Pour over potatoes; toss gently to coat. Serve warm. Yield: 4 servings (serving size: 3 potatoes).

*POINTS:* 3; **Exchanges:** 2 Starch
**Per serving:** CAL 163 (17% from fat); PRO 3.8g; FAT 3g (sat 0.6g); CARB 31.4g; FIB 3.1g; CHOL 0mg; IRON 2.2mg; SOD 45mg; CALC 23mg

**Make use of the mint in your garden with Mint-Glazed Potatoes and Minted-Molasses Pork Tenderloin, page 55.**

## Caraway Cabbage

1   teaspoon reduced-calorie stick margarine
Cooking spray
8   cups thinly sliced green cabbage
1   tablespoon chopped fresh parsley
1   teaspoon sugar
1   teaspoon chicken-flavored bouillon
    granules
¼ to ½ teaspoon freshly ground pepper
1   teaspoon caraway seeds

**1.** Melt margarine over medium heat in a large Dutch oven coated with cooking spray. Add cabbage and next 4 ingredients; cover and cook 5 minutes, stirring occasionally. Sprinkle with caraway seeds; cover and cook an additional 1 minute. Yield 6 servings (serving size: 1 cup).

*POINTS:* 0; **Exchanges:** 1 Veg
**Per serving:** CAL 37 (24% from fat); PRO 1.5g; FAT 1g (sat 0.1g); CARB 7.1g; FIB 2.8g; CHOL 0mg; IRON 0.8mg; SOD 163mg; CALC 57mg

## Cracked Pepper Linguine

Fat-free sour cream is the secret to this creamy, low-fat linguine.

1   (8-ounce) carton fat-free sour cream
1   tablespoon skim milk
1   tablespoon cracked pepper
1   tablespoon reduced-calorie stick margarine
¼   cup minced fresh onion
2   garlic cloves, minced
4   cups hot cooked linguine (about 8 ounces
    uncooked pasta), cooked without salt or fat
2   tablespoons (½ ounce) grated fresh
    Parmesan cheese
1½ tablespoons chopped fresh parsley

**1.** Combine sour cream, milk, and pepper in a small bowl; stir well, and set aside.

**2.** Melt margarine in a large nonstick skillet over medium heat. Add onion and garlic; sauté 3 minutes or until onion is crisp-tender. Remove from heat. Add pasta and sour cream mixture; toss well. Sprinkle with Parmesan cheese and parsley; serve immediately. Yield: 6 servings (serving size: ¾ cup).

*POINTS:* 4; **Exchanges:** 2 Starch, ½ Fat
**Per serving:** CAL 193 (11% from fat); PRO 8.6g; FAT 2.4g (sat 0.6g); CARB 32.8g; FIB 1.4g; CHOL 1mg; IRON 1.9mg; SOD 82mg; CALC 115mg

## Southwestern Rice

This simple side dish is a perfect accompaniment to Chicken Enchiladas, page 49, and Jicama-Orange Salad, page 76.

2   teaspoons cumin seeds
2   (16-ounce) cans one-third-less-salt chicken
    broth
2   cups uncooked long-grain rice
½   cup thinly sliced green onions

**1.** Place cumin seeds in a large saucepan, and cook over medium-high heat 3 minutes or until lightly browned, shaking pan frequently. Add broth, and bring to a boil. Add rice, and return to a boil. Cover, reduce heat, and simmer 25 minutes or until liquid is absorbed. Remove from heat, and stir in green onions. Yield: 8 servings (serving size: ¾ cup).

**Note:** You may substitute 2½ teaspoons ground cumin for cumin seeds, if desired (do not toast ground cumin).

*POINTS:* 3; **Exchanges:** 2½ Starch
**Per serving:** CAL 180 (2% from fat); PRO 5g; FAT 0.4g (sat 0.1g); CARB 38.2g; FIB 0.7g; CHOL 0mg; IRON 2.4mg; SOD 284mg; CALC 22mg

## Sweet Potato Sticks

Try these oven-fried potatoes with Sloppy Joes, page 13.

4   medium sweet potatoes (about 2 pounds),
    peeled
1   tablespoon vegetable oil
⅓   cup grated Parmesan cheese
Cooking spray

**1.** Preheat oven to 400°.

**2.** Cut potatoes lengthwise into ½-inch-thick slices. Cut slices into ¼-inch-wide strips. Place potato strips in a large bowl. Drizzle with oil and sprinkle with cheese; toss well. Arrange potato strips in a single layer on baking sheets coated with cooking spray. Bake at 400° for 35 minutes or until crisp and lightly browned, stirring every 10 minutes. Yield: 8 servings.

*POINTS:* 2; **Exchanges:** 1½ Starch, ½ Fat
**Per serving:** CAL 139 (20% from fat); PRO 3.1g; FAT 3.1g (sat 0.9g); CARB 25.1g; FIB 3.1g; CHOL 3mg; IRON 0.7mg; SOD 75mg; CALC 71mg

Cracked Pepper Linguine

Crispy Onion Rings and Steak With Ale, page 29, taste as good as your local steakhouse without all the fat.

## Crispy Onion Rings

Make sure you divide the cereal mixture in half before dredging the onion rings. Otherwise, the mixture will get soggy before all of the onion rings are coated.

2   large Vidalia or other sweet onions (about 1¼ pounds)
6   cups whole-wheat flake cereal (such as Wheaties), finely crushed
1   tablespoon chili powder
2   teaspoons sugar
1   teaspoon ground cumin
¼   teaspoon ground red pepper
1   cup egg substitute
Cooking spray

**1.** Preheat oven to 375°.

**2.** Cut each onion into 4 thick slices; separate into rings. Reserve small rings for another use. Set large rings aside.

**3.** Combine cereal, chili powder, sugar, cumin, and red pepper; stir well. Place half of cereal mixture in a shallow dish or pie plate. Set remaining half of mixture aside.

**4.** Beat egg substitute at high speed of a mixer until soft peaks form. Dip half of onion rings in egg substitute; dredge in crumb mixture in shallow dish. Place onion rings in a single layer on baking sheets coated with cooking spray. Place remaining half of cereal mixture in shallow dish; repeat procedure with remaining onion rings and egg substitute. Bake at 375° for 10 minutes or until crisp. Serve warm. Yield: 6 servings.

*POINTS:* 3; **Exchanges:** 2 Starch, ½ Very Lean Meat
**Per serving:** CAL 171 (6% from fat); PRO 8g; FAT 1.2g (sat 0.1g); CARB 34.4g; FIB 3.7g; CHOL 0mg; IRON 6.8mg; SOD 517mg; CALC 81mg

## Garlic-Herb-Cheese Grits

Plain grits get all dressed up in zesty garlic-spice cream cheese for this quick recipe. Stir it up in just 10 minutes.

2  (16-ounce) cans one-third-less-salt chicken broth
1  cup uncooked quick-cooking grits (not instant)
1  (6-ounce) tub light cream cheese with garlic and spices
¼  teaspoon freshly ground pepper

**1.** Bring broth to a boil in a medium saucepan over high heat; gradually stir in grits. Cook 5 minutes or until thick, stirring constantly. Remove from heat; stir in cream cheese and pepper. Serve immediately. Yield: 6 servings (serving size: ¾ cup).

*POINTS:* 4; *Exchanges:* 1½ Starch, 1 Fat
**Per serving:** CAL 170 (28% from fat); PRO 6.8g; FAT 5.2g (sat 3g); CARB 23.5g; FIB 1.3g; CHOL 20mg; IRON 1.7mg; SOD 182mg; CALC 39mg

## Cauliflower Medley

A zip-top plastic bag works great for marinating because once the air is squeezed out of the bag, the marinade coats the food and no stirring is required. You may use a large bowl instead, but remember to stir frequently so that the food gets evenly marinated.

8  cups fresh cauliflower florets
½  cup fat-free Italian dressing
2  tablespoons sliced ripe olives
2  tablespoons capers
¼  teaspoon cracked pepper
1  (4-ounce) jar diced pimiento, drained

**1.** Steam cauliflower, covered, 10 minutes or until crisp-tender.
**2.** Place cauliflower florets, dressing, olives, capers, pepper, and pimiento in a large zip-top plastic bag; seal and shake gently to coat cauliflower with dressing mixture. Marinate in refrigerator for at least 8 hours. Serve cauliflower with a slotted spoon. Yield: 8 servings (serving size: 1 cup).

*POINTS:* 0; *Exchanges:* 2 Veg
**Per serving:** CAL 51 (11% from fat); PRO 3.4g; FAT 0.6g (sat 0.1g); CARB 10.2g; FIB 3.8g; CHOL 0mg; IRON 0.9mg; SOD 432mg; CALC 38mg

## Oriental Crab Spread

⅓  cup tub-style light cream cheese
1  tablespoon low-salt soy sauce
1  teaspoon sugar
⅛  teaspoon white pepper
⅓  cup diced green bell pepper
1  tablespoon thinly sliced green onion
6  ounces lump crabmeat, shell pieces removed
1  (8-ounce) can whole water chestnuts, drained and coarsely chopped

**1.** Combine cream cheese, soy sauce, sugar, and white pepper in a medium bowl; beat at medium speed of a mixer until light and fluffy. Add remaining ingredients; stir well. Cover and chill. Serve with unsalted crackers. Yield: 8 servings (serving size: ¼ cup).

*POINTS:* 1; *Exchanges:* ½ Very Lean Meat, ½ Veg, ½ Fat
**Per serving:** CAL 56 (32% from fat); PRO 5.5g; FAT 2g (sat 1g); CARB 3.8g; FIB 0.2g; CHOL 27mg; IRON 0.5mg; SOD 163mg; CALC 36mg

## Spicy Lettuce Salad

¼  cup white vinegar
2  tablespoons minced fresh onion
1  tablespoon olive oil
½  teaspoon chili powder
⅛  teaspoon salt
1  garlic clove, crushed
16  cups torn iceberg lettuce

**1.** Combine first 6 ingredients in a large bowl; stir well with a whisk. Add lettuce; toss well. Yield: 8 servings (serving size: 2 cups).

*POINTS:* 1; *Exchanges:* 1 Veg
**Per serving:** CAL 26 (62% from fat); PRO 0.6g; FAT 1.8g (sat 0.2g); CARB 2g; FIB 0.6g; CHOL 0mg; IRON 0.4mg; SOD 44mg; CALC 12mg

## Ranch Slaw

This easy slaw pairs perfectly with Fiesta Burgers, page 49, and with Slow-Cooker Beef-and-Bean Burritos, page 26.

½  cup sliced green onions
2  (10-ounce) bags angel hair slaw
⅔  cup fat-free ranch dressing
2  (11-ounce) cans mandarin oranges in light syrup, well drained
1  ripe avocado, peeled, pitted, and coarsely chopped

1. Combine green onions and slaw in a large bowl. Add ranch dressing; toss to coat. Add mandarin oranges and chopped avocado; toss gently. Serve immediately. Yield: 12 servings (serving size: ¾ cup).

**Note:** Unless you plan to serve all of the slaw at one time, it's best to make half the recipe because it will water out if stored in the refrigerator for any length of time.

*POINTS:* 1; **Exchanges:** 1 Veg, ½ Fruit, ½ Fat
**Per serving:** CAL 69 (30% from fat); PRO 1.5g; FAT 2.3g (sat 0.4g); CARB 11.1g; FIB 0.9g; CHOL 0mg; IRON 0.7mg; SOD 168mg; CALC 54mg

### Garlic-Basil Squash

2  tablespoons chopped fresh basil
2  teaspoons olive oil
1  teaspoon water
¼  teaspoon salt
1  garlic clove, minced
4  small yellow squash, cut in half lengthwise (about ¾ pound)
4  medium zucchini, cut in half lengthwise (about 1½ pounds)
Cooking spray

1. Combine first 5 ingredients in a small bowl. Brush cut surfaces of yellow squash and zucchini with half of basil mixture; set aside.

2. Prepare grill. Place vegetables, cut sides down on grill rack coated with cooking spray, and grill 8 minutes or until vegetables are tender, turning and basting once with reserved marinade. Yield: 8 servings.

*POINTS:* 0; **Exchanges:** 1 Veg
**Per serving:** CAL 31 (38% from fat); PRO 1.5g; FAT 1.3g (sat 0.2g); CARB 4.5g; FIB 1.2g; CHOL 0mg; IRON 0.5mg; SOD 77mg; CALC 23mg

---

**Squash Smarts**

1. Zucchini and summer squash are best when they are young and small.

2. Choose squash that are free of soft spots and aren't dented or gashed.

3. Store squash in a plastic bag with holes in it in the refrigerator for up to three days.

---

### Honey Mustard-Whipped Sweet Potatoes

1  tablespoon margarine
½  cup sliced onion
3  medium sweet potatoes, peeled and cut into 1-inch pieces (about 1½ pounds)
1  cup low-salt chicken broth
1  tablespoon Dijon mustard
1  tablespoon honey
¼  teaspoon pepper

1. Melt margarine in a large saucepan over medium heat. Add onion and sweet potatoes; sauté 5 minutes. Add broth and remaining ingredients; bring to a boil. Cover, reduce heat, and simmer 20 minutes or until sweet potatoes are very tender.

2. Place sweet potato mixture in a food processor; process until smooth.

Yield: 4 servings (serving size: ¾ cup).

*POINTS:* 3; **Exchanges:** 2½ Starch
**Per serving:** CAL 198 (18% from fat); PRO 3.1g; FAT 4g (sat 0.7g); CARB 38.3g; FIB 4.3g; CHOL 0mg; IRON 1.2mg; SOD 187mg; CALC 34mg

### Mushroom Pilaf in Bell Pepper Cups

Serve with Herbed Pepper Steaks, page 50, and Garlic-Basil Squash (left). The red bell pepper wedges add color as well as vitamin C, but the pilaf may be served without them.

2  large red bell peppers
2  cups water
2  cups dried porcini mushrooms (about 2 ounces)
1  cup uncooked long-grain rice
¼  cup sliced green onions
½  teaspoon salt
Cooking spray

1. Cut each bell pepper into 4 wedges; discard seeds and membranes. Set peppers aside.

2. Bring 2 cups water to a boil in a medium saucepan; add mushrooms. Remove from heat; cover and let stand 15 minutes. Drain, reserving mushroom liquid. Chop mushrooms; set aside.

3. Add enough water to reserved mushroom liquid to measure 1 cup, and return to pan; bring to

a boil. Add rice; cover, reduce heat, and simmer 20 minutes. Add mushrooms, onions, and salt; cover and cook 1 minute. Set aside; keep warm.

**4.** Prepare grill. Place pepper wedges on grill rack coated with cooking spray; grill 8 minutes or just until tender. Spoon rice mixture evenly into bell pepper wedges. Yield: 8 servings (serving size: ½ cup rice and 1 bell pepper wedge).

*POINTS*: 2; **Exchanges**: 1½ Starch
**Per serving**: CAL 122 (2% from fat); PRO 2.6g; FAT 0.3g (sat 0.1g); CARB 26.1g; FIB 1.5g; CHOL 0mg; IRON 1.3mg; SOD 150mg; CALC 11mg

## Artichoke-Feta Green Salad

6   tablespoons fat-free Italian dressing
1   tablespoon red wine vinegar
¼   teaspoon dry mustard
1   cup frozen artichoke hearts, thawed
4   cups mixed baby salad greens
1   cup pear-shaped cherry tomatoes, halved
½   small red onion, sliced and separated into
     rings
¼   cup (1 ounce) crumbled feta cheese with
     basil and tomato

**1.** Combine first 3 ingredients in a large bowl; stir with a whisk. Stir in artichokes; marinate in refrigerator 1 hour. Add salad greens, tomatoes, and onion; toss gently. Place 1¼ cups salad on each of 4 plates; sprinkle each with 1 tablespoon cheese. Yield: 4 servings.

**Note:** Canned artichoke hearts may be substituted for frozen (with an increase in sodium), cherry tomatoes may be used instead of pear-shaped, and regular feta cheese may be substituted for basil-tomato feta.

*POINTS*: 2; **Exchanges**: 3 Veg, ½ Fat
**Per serving**: CAL 99 (21% from fat); PRO 5.7g; FAT 2.3g (sat 1.1g); CARB 16.4g; FIB 2.7g; CHOL 20mg; IRON 1.4mg; SOD 356mg; CALC 75mg

## Cheddar-Black Pepper Biscuits

2    cups all-purpose flour
1½   teaspoons baking powder
½    teaspoon coarsely ground pepper, divided
¼    teaspoon salt
2    tablespoons chilled stick margarine, cut
     into small pieces

¾   cup (3 ounces) shredded extra-sharp
    cheddar cheese
¾   cup skim milk
Cooking spray
1   large egg white, lightly beaten

**1.** Preheat oven to 425°.

**2.** Combine flour, baking powder, ¼ teaspoon pepper, and salt in a bowl; cut in margarine with a pastry blender or 2 knives until mixture resembles coarse meal. Add cheese; toss well. Add milk, stirring just until dry ingredients are moist.

**3.** Turn dough out onto a well-floured surface, and knead 4 or 5 times. Roll dough to ½-inch thickness; cut with a 2-inch decorative cookie cutter. Place biscuits 1 inch apart on baking sheets coated with cooking spray, and brush with egg white; sprinkle evenly with remaining ¼ teaspoon

**Herbed Pepper Steaks, page 50, Mushroom Pilaf in Bell Pepper Cups, Garlic-Basil Squash, and dinner rolls**

**Minted Cucumber-
Sprout Nests**

pepper. Bake at 425° for 15 minutes or until lightly browned. Yield: 1½ dozen (serving size: 1 biscuit).

*POINTS:* 2; **Exchanges:** 1 Starch, ½ Fat
**Per serving:** CAL 86 (31% from fat); PRO 3.2g; FAT 3g (sat 1.3g); CARB 11.3g; FIB 0.4g; CHOL 5mg; IRON 0.7mg; SOD 85mg; CALC 72mg

## Minted Cucumber-Sprout Nests

1    cup chopped cucumber
½    cup seeded chopped tomato
3    tablespoons lemon juice
1    teaspoon dried mint
¼    teaspoon salt
2    cups radish or alfalfa sprouts

**1.** Combine first 5 ingredients in a bowl, and toss gently. Arrange ½ cup sprouts on each of 4 plates, and top each with ⅓ cup cucumber mixture. Yield: 4 servings.

*POINTS:* 0; **Exchanges:** 1 Veg
**Per serving:** CAL 19 (14% from fat); PRO 1.6g; FAT 0.3g (sat 0g); CARB 3.8g; FIB 0.9g; CHOL 0mg; IRON 0.5mg; SOD 151mg; CALC 16mg

## Chili-Corn Mashed Potatoes

A hand-mixer works great for this recipe because the potatoes can be mashed in the saucepan without dirtying a bowl.

¾    cup frozen whole-kernel corn
2½   cups peeled cubed baking potato
3    tablespoons fat-free sour cream
3    tablespoons skim milk
1    tablespoon reduced-calorie stick margarine
½    teaspoon chili powder
¼    teaspoon salt
⅛    teaspoon ground cumin

**1.** Cook corn according to package directions, omitting salt; drain and set aside.

**2.** Place potato in a medium saucepan, and cover with water; bring to a boil. Cover, reduce heat, and simmer 10 minutes or until tender; drain. Return potato to pan; beat at medium speed of a mixer 1 minute. Add sour cream and next 5 ingredients; beat until smooth. Stir in corn. Yield: 4 servings (serving size: ¾ cup).

*POINTS:* 2; **Exchanges:** 1½ Starch, ½ Fat
**Per serving:** CAL 139 (15% from fat); PRO 4.2g; FAT 2.3g (sat 0.4g); CARB 26.8g; FIB 2.7g; CHOL 0mg; IRON 1mg; SOD 201mg; CALC 31mg

## Simple Sesame Spinach

Depending on the size of your Dutch oven, you may have to wilt the spinach in two batches. Divide the sesame seeds, lemon juice, and salt evenly between the batches.

3    (10-ounce) bags fresh spinach
Cooking spray
2    tablespoons sesame seeds, toasted
2    teaspoons lemon juice
½    teaspoon salt

**1.** Trim large stems from spinach. Wash spinach, and pat dry with paper towels.

**2.** Coat a large Dutch oven with cooking spray; place over medium heat until hot. Add spinach; cover and cook until spinach wilts, stirring occasionally. Remove from heat. Add sesame seeds, lemon juice, and salt; toss well. Yield: 8 servings (serving size: ½ cup).

*POINTS:* 0; **Exchanges:** 1 Veg, ½ Fat
**Per serving:** CAL 38 (40% from fat); PRO 3.7g; FAT 1.7g (sat 0.2g); CARB 4.1g; FIB 4.3g; CHOL 0mg; IRON 3.1mg; SOD 231mg; CALC 109mg

## Creamy Guacamole and Chips

To keep leftover guacamole from turning dark as quickly, save the pit from the avocado and press it into any leftover dip.

8    (6-inch) flour tortillas, each cut into 8 wedges
1½   cups peeled cubed avocado
1    cup fat-free ricotta cheese
⅓    cup coarsely chopped onion
2    tablespoons coarsely chopped fresh cilantro
2    tablespoons fresh lime juice
1    tablespoon seeded coarsely chopped jalapeño pepper
½    teaspoon salt

**1.** Preheat oven to 350°.

**2.** Place tortilla wedges on a baking sheet; bake at 350° for 10 minutes or until crisp. Set aside.

**3.** Place avocado and next 6 ingredients in a food processor; process until smooth. Serve with toasted tortilla wedges. Yield: 16 servings (serving size: 4 tortilla wedges and 2 tablespoons dip).

*POINTS:* 2; **Exchanges:** 1 Starch, ½ Fat
**Per serving:** CAL 90 (33% from fat); PRO 3.6g; FAT 3.3g (sat 0.6g); CARB 13.7g; FIB 0.8g; CHOL 2mg; IRON 0.6mg; SOD 83mg; CALC 41mg

### GROW YOUR OWN SPROUTS

Place alfalfa seeds in a wide-mouth quart-size jar, and add 1 cup warm water. Cover with cheesecloth; secure with a rubber band. Store in a dark, warm (about 70°) area 8 to 12 hours. Then rinse and drain seeds until water runs clear. Turn jar on its side, and shake to distribute seeds. Keep jar stored on its side and in indirect light. Rinse and drain sprouts daily. When sprouts have grown 1 to 2 inches (in three to five days), put jar in direct sunlight for several hours so they'll turn green. Then rinse sprouts before using or storing in refrigerator.

*Zucchini, a variety of summer squash, is available year-round but is most abundant during the summer months. This mild-flavored vegetable can be cooked with very delicate ingredients so the zucchini flavor comes through. Or the squash can be paired with bold flavors such as garlic and pungent herbs to bring them to life. Because zucchini contains a lot of water, the best cooking techniques are those that tend to dry the squash out. We recommend sautéeing, grilling, and baking.*

**To quickly slice zucchini into "half-moons" for our Okra, Tomato, and Zucchini Medley, cut zucchini in half lengthwise, and then cut into ¼-inch-thick slices.**

## Okra, Tomato, and Zucchini Medley

Cooking spray
1   small zucchini, halved lengthwise and sliced
1½  cups sliced fresh okra
2   tablespoons chopped onion
1   cup chopped tomato
1   teaspoon minced fresh or ¼ teaspoon dried basil
1   teaspoon minced fresh or ¼ teaspoon dried thyme
Dash of freshly ground pepper

**1.** Coat a large nonstick skillet with cooking spray; place over medium-high heat until hot. Add zucchini, okra, and onion; sauté 4 minutes. Stir in tomato and remaining ingredients. Cover, reduce heat to low, and simmer 5 minutes or until thoroughly heated. Yield: 4 servings (serving size: ½ cup).

**POINTS:** 0; **Exchanges:** 1 Veg
**Per serving:** CAL 31 (12% from fat); PRO 1.5g; FAT 0.4g (sat 0g); CARB 6.3g; FIB 1.3g; CHOL 0mg; IRON 0.7mg; SOD 8mg; CALC 35mg

## Pineapple-Date Dip

Serve this slightly sweet appetizer before a meal of roast chicken, pork, or lamb. Use scissors coated with cooking spray to chop the dates, or to save time, buy prechopped dates.

1   cup fat-free sour cream
1   cup frozen reduced-calorie frozen whipped topping, thawed
⅓   cup chopped pitted dates
1   (8-ounce) can unsweetened crushed pineapple, well drained
⅛   teaspoon ground nutmeg

**1.** Combine sour cream and whipped topping in a medium bowl; stir gently. Add dates and pineapple; stir gently. Cover and chill at least 1 hour, and sprinkle with nutmeg. Serve with fresh strawberries and apple wedges. Yield: 2 cups (serving size: 1 tablespoon).

**POINTS:** 0; **Exchanges:** Free
**Per serving:** CAL 17 (16% from fat); PRO 0.6g; FAT 0.3g (sat 0.2g); CARB 3.1g; FIB 0.2g; CHOL 0mg; IRON 0mg; SOD 7mg; CALC 3mg

## Jicama-Orange Salad

Juicy orange sections add contrasting texture and color to crisp strips of jicama and bell pepper in this toss-together salad. Serve with Chicken Enchiladas, page 49, and Southwestern Rice, page 68.

¼   cup white vinegar
1   tablespoon vegetable oil
½   teaspoon sugar
¼   teaspoon white pepper
¼   teaspoon chili powder
2   cups peeled julienne-cut jicama
1½  cups julienne-cut red bell pepper
4   large navel oranges, peeled and sectioned

**1.** Combine vinegar, vegetable oil, sugar, white pepper, and chili powder in a large bowl; stir with a whisk until vinaigrette is well blended. Add jicama, bell pepper, and orange sections, and toss gently to coat. Yield: 8 servings (serving size: ¾ cup).

**POINTS:** 1; **Exchanges:** ½ Fruit, ½ Fat
**Per serving:** CAL 54 (33% from fat); PRO 0.9g; FAT 2g (sat 0.4g); CARB 9.3g; FIB 2.5g; CHOL 0mg; IRON 0.6mg; SOD 3mg; CALC 21mg

## Speedy Caesar Salad

Slice the romaine lettuce leaves crosswise to include the rib. This adds a pleasant crunch to the salad.

6   cups sliced romaine lettuce
2   tablespoons grated Parmesan cheese
2   tablespoons water
2   tablespoons red wine vinegar
2   teaspoons olive oil
2   teaspoons anchovy paste
1   garlic clove, peeled
⅓   cup seasoned croutons

**1.** Place lettuce in a large bowl; set aside. Place Parmesan cheese and next 5 ingredients in a blender or food processor; process until well blended. Pour over lettuce, and toss well. Top with seasoned croutons. Yield: 5 servings (serving size: 1 cup).

**POINTS:** 1; **Exchanges:** 1 Veg, ½ Fat
**Per serving:** CAL 57 (52% from fat); PRO 2.8g; FAT 3.3g (sat 0.7g); CARB 3.9g; FIB 1.2g; CHOL 2mg; IRON 0.8mg; SOD 318mg; CALC 55mg

Okra, Tomato, and
Zucchini Medley

# Sweet Nothings

DONE RIGHT, DESSERT IS
A PIECE OF CAKE.

*I*n 1915, the average American woman spent five hours a day in the kitchen. Today, she spends an average of 15 minutes preparing the evening meal. In a way, it makes sense that homemade desserts have fallen by the wayside: Women have more commitments and less time. But then again, today's cooks have convenience products their grandmothers never dreamed of, time-saving culinary shortcuts such as cake mixes, frozen yogurt, and canned fruits that make preparing dessert as easy as pie (or brownies or cookies, for that matter). Dessert doesn't have to be difficult: It can be as simple as Cinnamon Crisps, which take less than 10 minutes to make, or Chocolate-Dipped Apricots, which call for a mere two ingredients. Nor does it have to be unhealthful. This chapter is filled with recipes that use low-fat ingredients and techniques to create more healthful versions of Grandmother's old stand-bys, including Pound Cake, and a few new classics, such as Kahlúa-Cinnamon Brownies and Capuccino Pudding Cake.*

**Serve Cherry-Yogurt Parfaits as a simple but elegant ending to any meal.**

Cappuccino
Pudding Cake

## Cappuccino Pudding Cake

1 cup all-purpose flour
⅔ cup granulated sugar
2 tablespoons unsweetened cocoa
2 teaspoons baking powder
¼ teaspoon salt
½ cup evaporated skim milk
1 teaspoon vegetable oil
1 teaspoon vanilla extract
¼ cup semisweet chocolate chips
1 cup firmly packed dark brown sugar
¼ cup unsweetened cocoa
1¾ cups hot water
2 (0.77-ounce) envelopes instant
  cappuccino coffee mix or ¼ cup other
  instant flavored coffee mix
9 tablespoons vanilla fat-free frozen yogurt

**1.** Preheat oven to 350°.

**2.** Combine first 5 ingredients in a 9-inch square baking pan; stir well. Stir in milk, oil, and vanilla. Stir in chocolate chips. Combine brown sugar and ¼ cup cocoa; sprinkle over batter. Combine hot water and coffee mix, stirring to dissolve. Pour coffee mixture over batter (do not stir). Bake at 350° for 40 minutes or until cake springs back when lightly touched in center. Serve warm with 1 tablespoon frozen yogurt on each serving. Yield: 9 servings.

*POINTS*: 5; **Exchanges:** 2½ Starch, 1 Fruit
**Per serving:** CAL 247 (11% from fat); PRO 4.2g; FAT 3g (sat 1.5g); CARB 52.4g; FIB 0.3g; CHOL 1mg; IRON 2mg; SOD 123mg; CALC 175mg

## Cherry-Yogurt Parfaits

2 teaspoons stick margarine
2 tablespoons chopped pecans
8 vanilla wafers, coarsely crushed
½ teaspoon ground cinnamon
1 (20-ounce) can light cherry pie filling, chilled
1 tablespoon brandy (optional)
2 (16-ounce) cartons vanilla low-fat yogurt
Fresh cherries with stems, frozen (optional)

**1.** Melt margarine over low heat in a small non-stick skillet. Add pecans; sauté 3 minutes or until toasted. Remove from heat; stir in cookie crumbs and cinnamon.

**2.** Combine pie filling and, if desired, brandy; stir well. Spoon 2 tablespoons pie filling mixture into each of 8 parfait glasses; top each with ¼ cup yogurt and 1½ teaspoons cookie mixture. Repeat layers; garnish with frozen cherries, if desired. Serve immediately. Yield: 8 servings.

*POINTS*: 4; **Exchanges:** 1 Fruit, ½ Sk Milk, ½ Starch, ½ Fat
**Per serving:** CAL 168 (25% from fat); PRO 6.3g; FAT 4.6g (sat 1.2g); CARB 26.1g; FIB 0.6g; CHOL 6mg; IRON 0.5mg; SOD 104mg; CALC 203mg

## Chewy Lemon Wafers

1 large egg white
¾ cup all-purpose flour
½ cup sugar
3 tablespoons stick margarine, melted
1 teaspoon grated lemon rind
½ teaspoon lemon extract
¼ teaspoon baking soda
¼ teaspoon ground cinnamon
⅛ teaspoon salt
Cooking spray

**1.** Preheat oven to 350°.

**2.** Place egg white in a medium bowl; beat with a whisk until foamy. Add flour and next 7 ingredients, stirring until smooth.

**3.** Drop by level teaspoonfuls onto baking sheets coated with cooking spray. Bake at 350° for 8 minutes or until edges are golden. Let cool completely on wire racks. Yield: 3 dozen (serving size: 1 cookie).

*POINTS*: 1; **Exchanges:** ½ Starch
**Per serving:** CAL 31 (29% from fat); PRO 0.4g; FAT 1g (sat 0.2g); CARB 5g; FIB 0.1g; CHOL 0mg; IRON 0.1mg; SOD 26mg; CALC 2mg

## Cinnamon Crisps

To evenly coat the tortillas, combine the sugar and cinnamon in an empty salt shaker.

1 tablespoon hot water
½ teaspoon vanilla extract
1½ tablespoons sugar
1 teaspoon ground cinnamon
4 (6-inch) flour tortillas
Cooking spray

**1.** Preheat oven to 400°.

**2.** Combine water and vanilla; stir well. Combine sugar and cinnamon; stir well. Coat both sides of tortillas with cooking spray. Brush both sides of tortillas with water mixture; sprinkle each side with sugar mixture.

**3.** Place tortillas on a wire rack; place wire rack in a jelly-roll pan. Bake at 400° for 6 minutes or until lightly browned. Yield: 4 servings.

*POINTS:* 3; **Exchanges:** 2 Starch
**Per serving:** CAL 144 (16% from fat); PRO 3.7g; FAT 2.5g (sat 0.3g); CARB 27.5g; FIB 1g; CHOL 0mg; IRON 1mg; SOD 0mg; CALC 34mg

### Chocolate-Dipped Apricots

One piece of this fruit has zero *POINTS,* but it is not a free food. Two pieces have 1 *POINT.*

2   ounces Swiss dark chocolate, chopped
1   (6-ounce) bag dried apricots

**1.** Place chocolate in a small microwave-safe bowl. Microwave, uncovered, at MEDIUM (50% power) 2 minutes or until softened, stirring until smooth. Dip each apricot halfway into chocolate; let excess chocolate drip off.

**2.** Place apricots on a wax paper-lined baking sheet; chill until set. Store in an airtight container in refrigerator up to 2 weeks. Yield: 34 servings.

*POINTS:* 0; **Exchanges:** ½ Fruit
**Per serving:** CAL 20 (32% from fat); PRO 0.3g; FAT 0.7g (sat 0.3g); CARB 3.7g; FIB 0.4g; CHOL 0mg; IRON 0.3mg; SOD 4mg; CALC 3mg

### Crunchy Fruit-and-Chocolate Drops

6   ounces milk chocolate, chopped, or ¾ cup milk chocolate chips
1   cup oven-toasted rice cereal (such as Rice Krispies)
½   cup nutlike cereal nuggets (such as Grape-Nuts)
⅓   cup golden raisins
⅓   cup finely chopped pitted prunes

**1.** Place chocolate in a medium microwave-safe bowl. Microwave at MEDIUM (50% power) 4 minutes or until softened, stirring after 2 minutes. Add cereals, raisins, and prunes, stirring until well blended.

**2.** Drop by heaping teaspoonfuls onto a wax paper-lined baking sheet; chill 1 hour or until firm. Store in an airtight container in refrigerator up to 2 days. Yield: 40 drops (serving size: 1 drop).

*POINTS:* 1; **Exchanges:** ½ Starch
**Per serving:** CAL 40 (32% from fat); PRO 0.6g; FAT 1.4g (sat 0.8g); CARB 6.4g; FIB 0.3g; CHOL 0mg; IRON 0.2mg; SOD 20mg; CALC 14mg

### Almond-Dusted Strawberries

1½ tablespoons slivered almonds, toasted
2½ ounces milk chocolate, coarsely chopped, or ⅓ cup milk chocolate chips
20  medium fresh strawberries (about 1 pint)

**1.** Place almonds in a zip-top plastic bag; finely crush with a rolling pin or meat mallet. Place crushed almonds in a bowl; set aside.

**2.** Place chocolate in a small microwave-safe bowl. Microwave at MEDIUM (50% power) 2 minutes or until softened, stirring until smooth. Dip each strawberry three-fourths of the way into chocolate; immediately dip tips of strawberries into crushed almonds. Place on a wax paper-lined baking sheet; chill 3 hours or until firm. Store in an airtight container in refrigerator up to 2 days. Yield: 20 servings.

*POINTS:* 1; **Exchanges:** ½ Fat
**Per serving:** CAL 27 (50% from fat); PRO 0.5g; FAT 1.5g (sat 0.7g); CARB 3.2g; FIB 0.5g; CHOL 0mg; IRON 0.1mg; SOD 3mg; CALC 10mg

Chocolate-Dipped Apricots, Crunchy Fruit-and-Chocolate Drops, and Almond-Dusted Strawberries

## Apple-Berry Crisp

2   medium cooking apples, peeled and thinly sliced
1   tablespoon lemon juice
Cooking spray
1   (10-ounce) package frozen raspberries in light syrup, thawed and undrained
1   cup regular oats
3   tablespoons reduced-calorie stick margarine, melted
2   tablespoons honey
1   teaspoon ground cinnamon
½   teaspoon ground nutmeg

**1.** Preheat oven to 375°.

**2.** Combine apples and lemon juice; toss gently. Place apple mixture in a 10- x 6-inch baking dish coated with cooking spray; top with raspberries.

**3.** Combine oats and next 4 ingredients in a small bowl; stir until well blended. Sprinkle oat mixture evenly over fruit mixture. Bake at 375° for 30 minutes or until apples are tender and oat mixture is lightly browned. Yield: 8 servings.

*POINTS:* 2; **Exchanges:** 1 Starch, ½ Fruit, ½ Fat
**Per serving:** CAL 139 (24% from fat); PRO 2g; FAT 3.7g (sat 0.5g); CARB 25.7g; FIB 4.6g; CHOL 0mg; IRON 1.6mg; SOD 42mg; CALC 29mg

## Moist Cranberry Coffee Cake

This cake has a sweet cranberry filling and a sprinkling of allspice, brown sugar, and oats—ingredients you probably have on hand.

½   cup reduced-calorie stick margarine, softened
⅔   cup granulated sugar
1   large egg
1   teaspoon vanilla extract
1¼  cups all-purpose flour
2   teaspoons baking powder
¼   cup skim milk
2   large egg whites
Cooking spray
1   cup whole-berry cranberry sauce
3   tablespoons granulated sugar
2   tablespoons regular oats
1   tablespoon brown sugar
¾   teaspoon ground allspice

**1.** Preheat oven to 350°.

**2.** Cream margarine, and gradually add ⅔ cup granulated sugar, beating well at medium speed of a mixer. Add egg and vanilla extract; beat well.

**3.** Combine flour and baking powder; stir well. Add flour mixture to creamed mixture alternately with milk, beginning and ending with flour mixture; beat well after each addition.

**4.** Beat egg whites at high speed of a mixer until stiff peaks form (do not overbeat). Gently fold egg whites into batter. Spoon half of batter into an 8-inch square baking pan coated with cooking spray. Combine cranberry sauce and 3 tablespoons granulated sugar; spoon over batter. Spoon remaining batter over cranberry mixture.

**5.** Combine oats, brown sugar, and allspice; sprinkle evenly over batter. Bake at 350° for 45 minutes or until a wooden pick inserted in center comes out clean. Let cool in pan on a wire rack 10 minutes. Serve warm. Yield: 9 servings.

*POINTS:* 6; **Exchanges:** 2½ Starch, ½ Fruit, 1 Fat
**Per serving:** CAL 264 (26% from fat); PRO 3.8g; FAT 7.5g (sat 0.2g); CARB 47.3g; FIB 0.8g; CHOL 25mg; IRON 1.2mg; SOD 130mg; CALC 79mg

**Moist Cranberry Coffee Cake doubles as a dessert and breakfast cake.**

## Ginger-Berry Shortcakes

1   cup fresh strawberry halves
2   tablespoons seedless raspberry jam
1   tablespoon cream sherry
⅛   teaspoon ground ginger
Dash of ground cinnamon
1   cup vanilla fat-free frozen yogurt
1   (4½-ounce) package ready-to-eat
    shortcakes (such as Dolly Madison)

**1.** Combine first 5 ingredients in a small bowl; stir well. Spoon ¼ cup frozen yogurt onto each shortcake; top each with ¼ cup strawberry mixture. Serve immediately. Yield: 4 servings.

*POINTS:* 4; **Exchanges:** 2 Starch, ½ Fruit
**Per serving:** CAL 197 (12% from fat); PRO 4.3g; FAT 2.7g (sat 0.5g); CARB 38.5g; FIB 2.5g; CHOL 16mg; IRON 1.1mg; SOD 163mg; CALC 56mg

## Crunchy Almond Creme

1   (8-ounce) carton vanilla low-fat yogurt
2   teaspoons amaretto (almond-flavored liqueur)
2   teaspoons slivered almonds, toasted
4   (1½-inch) amaretti cookies, crushed

**1.** Combine yogurt and amaretto in a small bowl; stir well. Spoon yogurt mixture evenly into 2 stemmed glasses. Sprinkle evenly with slivered almonds and cookie crumbs. Yield: 2 servings.

*POINTS:* 4; **Exchanges:** 2 Starch, 1 Fat
**Per serving:** CAL 193 (21% from fat); PRO 6.5g; FAT 4.6g (sat 1.6g); CARB 30g; FIB 0.8g; CHOL 7mg; IRON 0.5mg; SOD 106mg; CAL 212mg

## Creamy Amaretto Dip

Our test kitchens staff enjoyed this dip with fresh strawberries, sliced fresh peaches, and pears.

2   cups 1% low-fat cottage cheese
¾   cup sifted powdered sugar
¾   cup tub-style light cream cheese
¼   cup amaretto (almond-flavored liqueur)

**1.** Place all ingredients in a food processor; process until smooth. Pour into a bowl; cover and chill. Serve with fresh fruit. Yield: 48 servings (serving size: 1 tablespoon).

*POINTS:* 1; **Exchanges:** ½ Fat
**Per serving:** CAL 26 (24% from fat); PRO 1.5g; FAT 0.7g (sat 0.4g); CARB 2.7g; FIB 0g; CHOL 2mg; IRON 0mg; SOD 58mg; CALC 10mg

## Pink Grapefruit-and-Tarragon Sorbet

Grapefruit and tarragon may sound like an unlikely pair, but they are a match made in heaven in this exotic sorbet.

1½   cups sugar
1    cup water
2    (8-inch) tarragon sprigs, coarsely chopped
4    cups pink grapefruit juice
Tarragon sprigs (optional)

**1.** Combine sugar and water in a saucepan; cook over medium heat until sugar dissolves, stirring constantly. Add chopped tarragon; bring to a boil. Remove from heat; stir in grapefruit juice. Pour into a bowl; cover and chill at least 2 hours.

**2.** Pour mixture through a sieve into a 9-inch square baking pan; discard tarragon. Cover and freeze until firm.

**3.** Scoop sorbet into dessert dishes. Garnish with tarragon sprigs, if desired. Serve immediately. Yield: 10 servings (serving size: ½ cup).

*POINTS:* 3; **Exchanges:** 2½ Fruit, ½ Starch
**Per serving:** CAL 173 (0% from fat); PRO 0.5g; FAT 0.1g (sat 0g); CARB 43.9g; FIB 0g; CHOL 0mg; IRON 2mg; SOD 1mg; CALC 9mg

## Lemon-Poppy Seed Cake

1   cup egg substitute
½   cup granulated sugar
⅓   cup vegetable oil
¼   cup water
3   tablespoons lemon juice
1   (18.25-ounce) package light yellow cake mix (such as Betty Crocker)
1   (8-ounce) carton vanilla fat-free yogurt
2   tablespoons poppy seeds
Cooking spray
½   cup sifted powdered sugar
2   tablespoons lemon juice

**1.** Preheat oven to 350°.

**2.** Combine first 7 ingredients in a large bowl; beat at medium speed of a mixer 6 minutes. Stir in poppy seeds.

**3.** Pour batter into a 10-cup Bundt pan coated with cooking spray. Bake at 350° for 50 minutes or until a wooden pick inserted in center comes

Pink Grapefruit-and-Tarragon Sorbet

Frozen Chocolate
Brownie Pie

out clean. Let cool in pan on a wire rack 10 minutes; remove from pan.

**4.** Combine powdered sugar and 2 tablespoons lemon juice, and stir well. Brush cake with glaze, and let cool completely. Yield: 24 servings (serving size: 1 slice).

*POINTS*: 4; **Exchanges**: 1½ Starch, ½ Fruit, ½ Fat
**Per serving**: CAL 171 (32% from fat); PRO 1.6g; FAT 6g (sat 1.3g); CARB 28.8g; FIB 0g; CHOL 0mg; IRON 0.6mg; SOD 22mg; CALC 49mg

## Frozen Chocolate Brownie Pie

Your guests will never believe that this make-ahead dessert is actually healthful.

⅔ cup firmly packed brown sugar
¼ cup stick margarine
⅓ cup unsweetened cocoa
¼ cup all-purpose flour
¼ teaspoon salt
½ cup egg substitute
¼ cup low-fat buttermilk
1 teaspoon vanilla extract
Cooking spray
8 cups vanilla fat-free frozen yogurt, softened and divided
4 cups chocolate fat-free frozen yogurt, softened
¾ cup chocolate-flavored syrup
Fresh strawberry halves (optional)

**1.** Preheat oven to 350°.

**2.** Combine brown sugar and margarine in a large saucepan; cook over medium heat until sugar dissolves, stirring constantly. Remove from heat; let cool slightly.

**3.** Combine cocoa, flour, and salt in a medium bowl; gradually add egg substitute and buttermilk, stirring until blended. Stir in margarine mixture and vanilla. Pour batter into a 9-inch springform pan coated with cooking spray. Bake at 350° for 15 minutes. Let cool in pan on a wire rack.

**4.** Spread 4 cups vanilla yogurt over cooled brownie layer; freeze at least 30 minutes or until firm. Spread chocolate yogurt over vanilla yogurt; freeze at least 30 minutes or until firm. Spread remaining 4 cups vanilla yogurt over chocolate yogurt. Cover and freeze at least 8 hours. Cut pie

into 12 wedges; drizzle each serving with 1 tablespoon chocolate syrup. Garnish with strawberry halves, if desired. Yield: 12 servings.

*POINTS*: 7; **Exchanges**: 3 Starch, 1 Fruit
**Per serving**: CAL 319 (12% from fat); PRO 9.1g; FAT 4.4g (sat 1g); CARB 62.4g; FIB 0.5g; CHOL 0mg; IRON 1.3mg; SOD 252mg; CALC 252mg

## Layered Ambrosia

You'll want to serve this dessert during the cold days of winter, when you can enjoy the fresh citrus at its juicy best.

3 cups fresh orange sections, divided
1 cup fresh pink grapefruit sections
½ cup flaked sweetened coconut, divided
1 (8-ounce) can unsweetened crushed pineapple, undrained
3 tablespoons honey

**1.** Arrange half of orange sections in a medium glass bowl; top with grapefruit sections, ¼ cup coconut, pineapple, and remaining orange sections. Drizzle with honey, and sprinkle with remaining ¼ cup coconut. Cover and chill 8 hours. Yield: 10 servings (serving size: about ½ cup).

*POINTS*: 1; **Exchanges**: 1½ Fruit
**Per serving**: CAL 88 (17% from fat); PRO 0.9g; FAT 1.7g (sat 1.5g); CARB 19g; FIB 2.9g; CHOL 0mg; IRON 0.2mg; SOD 13mg; CALC 30mg

## Pineapple-Cheese Pudding

2 cups 1% low-fat cottage cheese
1 tablespoon stick margarine, melted
½ teaspoon vanilla extract
3 large egg whites or ½ cup egg substitute
⅓ cup sugar
2 tablespoons all-purpose flour
1 (8-ounce) can unsweetened crushed pineapple, drained
Cooking spray
⅛ teaspoon ground cinnamon

**1.** Preheat oven to 425°.

**2.** Place first 4 ingredients in a food processor; process 10 seconds. Add sugar, flour, and pineapple; process 10 seconds.

**3.** Pour pineapple mixture into a 10- x 6-inch baking dish coated with cooking spray, and sprinkle with cinnamon. Place baking dish in a 13- x

*S*plitting cake layers evenly can be a difficult task. But it doesn't have to be. With these tips, and a little extra care, you can acheive near-professional results with minimal fuss.

**1** To slice a cake in half evenly, insert toothpicks around the outside, marking the middle. Using a serrated knife, slice into the cake about 2 inches, using the toothpicks as a guide.

**2** Wrap a long piece of dental floss around layer, placing over cut; tie floss once. Slowly tighten the floss—it will make a clean, even cut through the cake layer, dividing it in half.

9-inch baking pan, and add water to pan to a depth of 1-inch.

**4.** Bake at 425° for 10 minutes; reduce oven temperature to 350°. Bake at 350° for 40 minutes or until a knife inserted near center comes out clean. Serve warm or at room temperature. Yield: 6 servings (serving size: ⅔ cup).

**POINTS:** 3; **Exchanges:** 1 Very Lean Meat, 1 Fruit, ½ Starch, ½ Fat
**Per serving:** CAL 150 (17% from fat); PRO 11.4g; FAT 2.8g (sat 0.9g); CARB 19.6g; FIB 0.4g; CHOL 3mg; IRON 0.3mg; SOD 354mg; CALC 53mg

## Raspberry-Chocolate Soda

1½ cups fresh raspberries
4   teaspoons sugar
2   cups raspberry-flavored or plain sparkling water, chilled
1   cup chocolate low-fat ice cream

**1.** Place raspberries and sugar in a food processor, and process 15 seconds or until smooth. Strain raspberry purée through a sieve into a bowl, and discard seeds.

**2.** Combine 2 tablespoons raspberry purée and ½ cup sparkling water in each of 4 glasses; stir gently. Add ¼ cup ice cream to each glass. Serve immediately. Yield: 4 servings.

**POINTS:** 2; **Exchanges:** 1 Starch
**Per serving:** CAL 94 (17% from fat); PRO 1.9g; FAT 1.8g (sat 0.8g); CARB 18.5g; FIB 0g; CHOL 5mg; IRON 0.3mg; SOD 0mg; CALC 60mg

## Strawberry-Yogurt Layer Cake

Store-bought products make this cake simple to prepare, but it's impressive enough for company.

1   (18.25-ounce) package reduced-fat white cake mix (such as Betty Crocker Sweet Rewards)
Cooking spray
8   cups strawberry fat-free frozen yogurt, softened
3   cups frozen reduced-calorie whipped topping, thawed
Fresh strawberries (optional)

**1.** Prepare and bake cake mix according to package directions, using 2 (9-inch) round cake pans coated with cooking spray. Let cake cool in pans

on wire racks 10 minutes. Remove from pans; let cool completely on wire racks.

**2.** Split cake layers in half horizontally using a serrated knife or a long piece of dental floss; place 1 bottom layer, cut side up, on a freezer-safe cake plate. Spread with one-third of yogurt, and freeze. Repeat procedure with remaining cake layers and yogurt, ending with a cake layer. Cover and freeze at least 3 hours. Spread whipped topping on top and sides of cake; cover loosely, and freeze until firm. Let stand at room temperature 5 to 10 minutes before slicing. Serve frozen. Garnish with strawberries, if desired. Yield: 14 servings (serving size: 1 slice).

**POINTS:** 7; **Exchanges:** 3 Starch, 1 Fruit, ½ Fat
**Per serving:** CAL 327 (21% from fat); PRO 5.3g; FAT 7.5g (sat 1.3g); CARB 58.5g; FIB 0.1g; CHOL 0mg; IRON 0.6mg; SOD 313mg; CALC 157mg

## Kahlúa-Cinnamon Brownies

¼   cup semisweet chocolate chips
¼   cup reduced-calorie stick margarine
¼   cup Kahlúa (coffee-flavored liqueur)
2   teaspoons vanilla extract
¾   cup all-purpose flour
¼   cup unsweetened cocoa
1   teaspoon ground cinnamon
¾   teaspoon baking powder
¼   teaspoon salt
⅔   cup firmly packed brown sugar
1   large egg
Cooking spray
1   teaspoon sugar

**1.** Preheat oven to 350°.

**2.** Combine chocolate chips and margarine in a small saucepan; cook over medium-low heat until chocolate melts, stirring constantly. Remove from heat; stir in Kahlúa and vanilla. Set aside.

**3.** Combine flour and next 4 ingredients in a small bowl; stir well, and set aside.

**4.** Combine brown sugar and egg in a large bowl; beat at low speed of a mixer until blended. Add chocolate mixture, and beat well. Add flour mixture, and beat until well blended. Pour batter into an 8-inch square baking pan coated with cooking spray. Bake at 350° for 30 minutes or until a wooden pick inserted in center comes out clean. Remove from oven; immediately sprinkle granulated sugar over brownies. Let cool completely in pan on a wire rack. Yield: 16 servings (serving size: 1 brownie).

**POINTS:** 2; **Exchanges:** 1 Starch, ½ Fat
**Per serving:** CAL 99 (27% from fat); PRO 1.5g; FAT 3g (sat 1g); CARB 16.9g; FIB 0.2g; CHOL 13mg; IRON 0.9mg; SOD 93mg; CALC 24mg

## Pound Cake

Cooking spray
1   teaspoon cake flour
⅔   cup sugar
½   cup stick margarine, softened
3   large egg whites or ½ cup egg substitute
1   tablespoon vanilla extract
1   teaspoon almond extract
2½  cups sifted cake flour
¾   teaspoon baking soda
¼   teaspoon salt
1   (8-ounce) carton vanilla low-fat yogurt

**1.** Preheat oven to 350°.

**2.** Coat an 8½- x 4½-inch loaf pan with cooking spray; dust with 1 teaspoon cake flour, and set aside.

**3.** Beat sugar and margarine at medium speed of a mixer until light and fluffy (about 5 minutes). Add egg whites; beat 4 minutes or until well blended. Add extracts, and beat at low speed until well blended.

**4.** Combine 2½ cups flour, baking soda, and salt in a bowl; stir well. Add flour mixture to creamed mixture alternately with yogurt, beginning and ending with flour mixture.

**5.** Pour batter into prepared pan. Bake at 350° for 1 hour and 5 minutes or until a wooden pick inserted in center comes out clean. Let cool in pan 10 minutes; remove from pan. Let cool completely on a wire rack. Serve plain or topped with fruit. Yield: 16 servings (serving size: 1 slice).

**POINTS:** 4; **Exchanges:** 1½ Starch, 1 Fat
**Per serving:** CAL 157 (34% from fat); PRO 2.5g; FAT 6g (sat 1.6g); CARB 22.7g; FIB 0g; CHOL 1mg; IRON 0.1mg; SOD 161mg; CALC 38mg

## Orange Sherbet Terrine Cake

1   (16-ounce) round angel food cake
2   cups orange sherbet, softened
⅔   cup chocolate-flavored syrup
1   tablespoon Kahlúa (coffee-flavored liqueur)
½   teaspoon grated orange rind
24  fresh orange sections
Orange rind curls (optional)

**1.** Slice off top third of cake, using a serrated knife; set aside. Hollow out bottom portion of cake, leaving a 1½-inch-wide cavity, making sure not to cut through bottom of cake; reserve torn cake for another use.

This Pound Cake has so much flavor, you won't even miss the pound of butter.

**2.** Pack sherbet into cavity of cake, pressing firmly with back of a spoon; replace top of cake. Wrap in heavy-duty plastic wrap, and freeze at least 8 hours. Let cake stand at room temperature 5 to 10 minutes before slicing.

**3.** Combine chocolate syrup, Kahlúa, and orange rind; stir well.

**4.** Cut cake into 12 slices. Drizzle chocolate mixture evenly over each slice. Top each slice with 2 orange sections. Garnish with orange rind curls, if desired. Yield: 12 servings.

*POINTS:* 4; **Exchanges:** 1½ Fruit, 1 Starch
**Per serving:** CAL 187 (8% from fat); PRO 2.6g; FAT 1.6g (sat 0.4g); CARB 40.7g; FIB 0.8g; CHOL 2mg; IRON 0.7mg; SOD 105mg; CALC 72mg

### Peaches Amaretto

8   cups peeled sliced fresh peaches (about 3 pounds)
½   cup amaretto (almond-flavored liqueur)
8   (1½-inch) amaretti cookies, crushed

**1.** Combine peaches and amaretto in a large shallow dish; stir well. Cover and chill 2 hours, stirring occasionally. Spoon peaches and amaretto evenly into 8 dessert compotes; sprinkle evenly with crushed cookies. Yield: 8 servings.

*POINTS:* 2; **Exchanges:** 2 Fruit, ½ Fat
**Per serving:** CAL 146 (5% from fat); PRO 1.6g; FAT 0.8g (sat 0.2g); CARB 27.7g; FIB 2.9g; CHOL 0mg; IRON 0.4mg; SOD 0mg; CALC 11mg

### Raspberry Chess Custard

Cornmeal creates a thin, slightly crunchy top layer on the custard filling.

Cooking spray
48  fresh raspberries
⅔   cup sugar
1   tablespoon all-purpose flour
1   tablespoon yellow cornmeal
1   cup skim milk
⅔   cup low-fat buttermilk
2   tablespoons stick margarine, melted
3   large egg whites, lightly beaten
1   large egg, lightly beaten

**1.** Preheat oven to 350°.

**2.** Coat 6 (6-ounce) custard cups with cooking spray. Place 8 raspberries in the bottom of each cup; set aside.

**3.** Combine sugar, flour, and cornmeal in a bowl. Stir in skim milk and next 4 ingredients; pour into prepared custard cups.

**4.** Place custard cups in a 13- x 9-inch baking pan. Add hot water to pan to a depth of 1-inch. Bake at 350° for 30 minutes or until a knife inserted near center comes out clean. Remove cups from water; let cool slightly on a wire rack. Serve warm. Yield: 6 servings.

*POINTS:* 4; **Exchanges:** 1½ Starch, ½ Fruit, 1 Fat
**Per serving:** CAL 194 (24% from fat); PRO 6.6g; FAT 5.2g (sat 1.2g); CARB 30.8g; FIB 1.2g; CHOL 40mg; IRON 0.4mg; SOD 163mg; CALC 127mg

### Fruit-and-Cookie Pizzas

Store the remaining cookie dough in the freezer so you can make this dessert at any time.

1   (18-ounce) package refrigerated sugar cookie dough
¼   cup light ricotta cheese
1   teaspoon sifted powdered sugar
⅛   teaspoon vanilla extract
2   canned peach slices in juice, drained and cut into very thin slices
1   small kiwifruit, peeled and thinly sliced
2   teaspoons reduced-sugar apricot spread, melted

**1.** Preheat oven to 350°.

**2.** Cut 2 (½-inch-thick) slices from dough; reserve remaining dough for another use. Gently press each slice into a 4-inch circle on a baking sheet. Bake at 350° for 10 minutes or until golden. Let cool on pan 1 minute, and carefully remove from pan. Let cookies cool completely on a wire rack.

**3.** Combine cheese, powdered sugar, and vanilla extract in a bowl, and stir well. Spread cheese mixture evenly over each cookie, and top with sliced peaches and kiwifruit. Brush each pizza with melted apricot spread . Serve immediately. Yield: 2 servings.

*POINTS:* 4; **Exchanges:** 1½ Starch, 1 Fat, ½ Fruit
**Per serving:** CAL 188 (32% from fat); PRO 5.2g; FAT 6.6g (sat 3.1g); CARB 26.6g; FIB 1.4g; CHOL 4mg; IRON 0.1mg; SOD 149mg; CALC 40mg

Fruit-and-Cookie Pizzas

| FOOD | WEIGHT (OR COUNT) | YIELD |
|---|---|---|
| Apples | 1 pound (3 medium) | 3 cups sliced |
| Bananas | 1 pound (3 medium) | 2½ cups sliced or about 2 cups mashed |
| Bread | 1 pound | 12 to 16 slices |
| | About 1½ slices | 1 cup fresh breadcrumbs |
| Cabbage | 1 pound head | 4½ cups shredded |
| Carrots | 1 pound | 3 cups shredded |
| Cheese, American or cheddar | 1 pound | About 4 cups shredded |
| cottage | 1 pound | 2 cups |
| cream | 3- ounce package | 6 tablespoons |
| Chocolate chips | 6- ounce package | 1 cup |
| Cocoa | 1 pound | 4 cups |
| Coconut, flaked or shredded | 1 pound | 5 cups |
| Coffee | 1 pound | 80 tablespoons (40 cups perked) |
| Corn | 2 medium ears | 1 cup kernels |
| Cornmeal | 1 pound | 3 cups |
| Crab, in shell | 1 pound | ¾ to 1 cup flaked |
| Crackers, chocolate wafers | 19 wafers | 1 cup crumbs |
| graham crackers | 14 squares | 1 cup crumbs |
| saltine crackers | 28 crackers | 1 cup crumbs |
| vanilla wafers | 22 wafers | 1 cup crumbs |
| Dates, pitted | 1 pound | 3 cups chopped |
| | 8- ounce package | 1½ cups chopped |
| Eggs | 4 large | 1 cup |
| whites | 8 to 11 | 1 cup |
| yolks | 12 to 14 | 1 cup |
| Flour, all-purpose | 1 pound | 3½ cups |
| cake | 1 pound | 4¾ to 5 cups sifted |
| whole-wheat | 1 pound | 3½ cups unsifted |
| Green bell pepper | 1 large | 1 cup diced |
| Lemon | 1 medium | 2 to 3 tablespoons juice; 2 teaspoons grated rind |
| Lettuce | 1- pound head | 6¼ cups torn |
| Lime | 1 medium | 1½ to 2 tablespoons juice; 1½ teaspoons grated rind |
| Macaroni | 4 ounces dry (1 cup) | 2 cups cooked |
| Margarine | 1 pound | 2 cups |
| | ¼- pound stick | ½ cup |
| Marshmallows | 10 large | 1 cup |
| | 10 miniature | 1 large marshmallow |
| | ½ pound miniature | 4½ cups |
| Milk, evaporated, skim | 12- ounce can | 1½ cups |

| FOOD | WEIGHT (OR COUNT) | YIELD |
|---|---|---|
| Milk, continued | | |
| sweetened, condensed, fat-free | | |
| or low-fat | 14- ounce can | 1¼ cups |
| Mushrooms | 3 cups raw (8 ounces) | 1 cup sliced cooked |
| Nuts, almonds | 1 pound | 1 to 1¾ cups nutmeats |
| | 1 pound shelled | 3½ cups nutmeats |
| peanuts | 1 pound | 2¼ cups nutmeats |
| | 1 pound shelled | 3 cups |
| pecans | 1 pound | 2¼ cups nutmeats |
| | 1 pound shelled | 4 cups |
| walnuts | 1 pound | 1⅔ cups nutmeats |
| | 1 pound shelled | 4 cups |
| Oats, quick-cooking | 1 cup | 1¾ cups cooked |
| Onion | 1 medium | ½ cup chopped |
| Orange | 1 medium | ½ cup juice; 2 tablespoons grated rind |
| Peaches | 2 medium | 1 cup sliced |
| Pears | 2 medium | 1 cup sliced |
| Potatoes, baking | 3 medium | 2 cups cubed cooked or 1¾ cups mashed |
| sweet | 3 medium | 3 cups sliced |
| Raisins | 1 pound | 3 cups |
| Rice, long-grain | 1 cup | 3 to 4 cups cooked |
| quick-cooking | 1 cup | 2 cups cooked |
| Shrimp, raw in shell | 1½ pounds | 2 cups (¾ pound) cleaned, cooked |
| Spaghetti | 7 ounces | About 4 cups cooked |
| Strawberries | 1 quart | 4 cups sliced |
| Sugar, brown | 1 pound | 2⅓ cups firmly packed |
| powdered | 1 pound | 3½ cups unsifted |
| granulated | 1 pound | 2 cups |

## EQUIVALENT MEASURES

| | | | | | | |
|---|---|---|---|---|---|---|
| 3 | teaspoons | 1 tablespoon | | 2 | cups | 1 pint (16 fluid ounces) |
| 4 | tablespoons | ¼ cup | | 4 | cups | 1 quart |
| 5⅓ | tablespoons | ⅓ cup | | 4 | quarts | 1 gallon |
| 8 | tablespoons | ½ cup | | ⅛ | cup | 2 tablespoons |
| 16 | tablespoons | 1 cup | | ⅓ | cup | 5 tablespoons plus 1 teaspoon |
| 2 | tablespoons (liquid) | 1 ounce | | ⅔ | cup | 10 tablespoons plus 2 teaspoons |
| 1 | cup | 8 fluid ounces | | ¾ | cup | 12 tablespoons |

**ale** A robustly flavored beer. It is somewhat bitter and varies in color from light to dark amber.

**allspice** A pea-size berry from the pimiento tree, named because it tastes like a combination of cloves, cinnamon, and nutmeg. It can be purchased as whole berries or ground, and is used in both savory and sweet dishes.

**amaretto** An almond-flavored liqueur originally from Italy.

**anchovy paste** A combination of ground anchovy fillets, vinegar, spices, and water that is packaged in tubes.

**balsamic vinegar** An Italian vinegar made from white Trebbiano grapes. Aged over a period of years in wooden barrels, the vinegar has a dark color and pungent sweetness.

**cake flour** A soft-wheat flour with a fine texture and high starch content. Also called pastry flour, it is used to produce very tender cakes and pastries.

**capers** A flower bud from a Mediterranean bush. The buds are picked, dried, and pickled in a salty vinegar brine.

**cilantro** The fresh leaves from the coriander plant. Widely used in Asian and Latin American cooking, it has a pungent flavor that lends itself to spicy foods.

**couscous** Made from semolina, a coarsely ground durum wheat. This staple of North African dining takes just five minutes to prepare and can be used much like rice.

**curry powder** A traditional Indian blend of up to 20 herbs, spices, and seeds. It is available in two degrees of spiciness: standard and hot (Madras).

**Feta cheese** A classic white and crumbly Greek cheese with a rich, tangy flavor. Traditionally made with sheep's or goat's milk.

**five-spice powder** A mixture of five ground spices usually consisting of cinnamon, cloves, fennel seed, star anise, and Szechuan peppercorns. This spice is used frequently in Chinese cooking.

**ginger** A common spice known for its peppery and sweet flavor. Ginger comes in several forms: fresh (the gnarled root), dried ground, crystallized, bottled chopped, and pickled.

**hoisin sauce** A thick, sweet, and spicy Asian sauce. It is a mixture of soybeans, garlic, chile peppers, and other spices. It keeps indefinitely in the refrigerator.

**hominy** Dried corn kernels that have had the hull and germ removed. Hominy is available dried or, more frequently, canned.

**jicama** A root vegetable popular in Latin American countries. Eaten raw or cooked, it has a sweet flavor and crunchy flesh.

**julienne** To cut into thin matchsticklike strips, especially vegetables.

**kiwifruit** A small oblong fruit that has a rough brown covering on the outside and bright-green flesh flecked with tiny edible black seeds inside. Eaten peeled, the fruit tastes similar to pineapple and strawberry.

**mango** A juicy and exotically sweet fruit with fragrant, golden flesh. The flesh must be carefully carved away from the huge flat seed that traverses the length of the fruit.

**Marsala** A fortified Italian wine from Sicily. It has a rich flavor that varies from dry to sweet and is used as a dessert wine as well as in many recipes.

**molasses** The brownish-black syrup produced during the refining of sugar cane and sugar beets.

**paprika** A common seasoning made from sweet red pepper pods; its flavor ranges from mild to hot.

**pearl barley** A hulled form of the grain barley. It comes in three sizes—coarse, medium, and fine—and is a common ingredient in many soups and stews.

**porcini mushroom** A wild mushroom with a meaty texture and an earthy flavor. It is typically available dried.

**sesame oil** An oil expressed from sesame seeds. Sesame oil comes in two basic types: light and dark. The light is yellow with a mild nutty flavor; the dark has a much stronger flavor and fragrance. Sesame oil is frequently used in Asian dishes.

**shallot** A plant related to the onion but formed with a divided bulb like garlic. The shallot has a mild onion flavor.

**shiitake mushroom** A mushroom with a full-bodied, meaty flavor. The tough stem should be removed.

## Nutrition and Serving-Size Information

Here are some specific guidelines *Weight Watchers* Magazine adheres to regarding our recipes. For nutritional accuracy, please follow our suggestions.

• When preparing a recipe that yields more than one serving, it is important to mix the ingredients well and then divide the mixture evenly.

• Where liquid and solid parts have to be divided evenly, drain the liquid and set it aside. Evenly divide the remaining ingredients; then add equal amounts of the liquid to each serving.

• Unless otherwise indicated, selections of meat, poultry, and fish refer to cooked, skinned, and boned servings.

• The selection information is designated as follows: P/M (Protein/Milk), FA (Fat), FR/V (Fruit/Vegetable), B (Bread), C (Bonus Calories).

• The selection information no longer contains fractions: B, FR/V, and FA are rounded up if 0.5 or above; P/M is rounded up if 0.75 or above; and C only includes bonus calories above 30. If all of the selections are rounded up, bonus calories are decreased; if all of the selections are rounded down, bonus calories are increased.

• Recipes also provide approximate nutritional data, including the following: cal (calories), pro (protein), fat (total fat), sat (saturated fat), carb (carbohydrates), fib (dietary fiber), chol (cholesterol), iron (iron), sod (sodium), calc (calcium). Measurements are abbreviated as follows: g (grams), mg (milligrams).

**Note:** Because data on fat distribution are not available for some processed foods, these breakdowns should be considered approximate.

• Recipes include *POINTS*® based on Weight Watchers International's 1•2•3 Success® Weight Loss Plan. (Please turn to page 3 for more information about this plan.)

• *POINTS* are calculated from a formula based on calories, fat, and fiber that assigns higher points to higher-calorie, higher-fat foods. Based on your present weight, you are allowed a certain amount of *POINTS* per day.

• The recipes that are shown in our photographs may vary as to the number of servings pictured. It is important that you refer to the recipes for the exact serving information.

## U S E F U L   E Q U I V A L E N T S   F O R   L I Q U I D   I N G R E D I E N T S   B Y   V O L U M E

|  | Fahrenheit | Celsius | Gas Mark |
|---|---|---|---|
| **Freeze Water** | 32° F | 0°C | |
| **Room Temperature** | 68° F | 20° C | |
| **Boil Water** | 212° F | 100° C | |
| **Bake** | 325° F | 160° C | 3 |
| | 350° F | 180° C | 4 |
| | 375° F | 190° C | 5 |
| | 400° F | 200° C | 6 |
| | 425° F | 220° C | 7 |
| | 450° F | 230° C | 8 |
| **Broil** | | | Grill |

# RECIPE INDEX